· MEREHURST ·
EMBROIDERY SKILLS

NEEDLELACE

· MEREHURST ·
EMBROIDERY SKILLS

NEEDLELACE

Pat Earnshaw

MEREHURST
LONDON

Published 1991 by Merehurst Limited
Ferry House
51–57 Lacy Road
Putney
London SW15 1PR

A catalogue record for this book is
available from the British Library.

Project Editor: Polly Boyd
Edited by Diana Brinton
Designed by Bill Mason
Photography by Stewart Grant (except pages 6, 8, 9, 11,
29, 105, 111, 113, 116–117, 118, 119, 124–125)
Artworks by Lindsay Blow
Typesetting by Rowland Phototypesetting Limited,
Bury St Edmunds, Suffolk
Colour Separation by
Fotographics Limited, UK–Hong Kong
Printed in Italy by
New Interlitho S.p.a., Milan

CONTENTS

Introduction   6

Chapter One: BASIC EQUIPMENT AND SKILLS   10

Chapter Two: STITCHES FROM TRADITIONAL LACES   28

   Point de France   30

   Point de Sedan   44

   Argentan   52

   Argentella   62

   Alençon   74

   Réseau Venise   84

   Point de gaze   94

Chapter Three: DESIGNS: TRADITIONAL AND ONWARDS   104

Index   127

INTRODUCTION

Needlelace is a form of embroidery with the cloth taken away, the needle and thread making loops in the air, and the stitches passing through nothing except themselves. The basic looping, which is simplicity itself, is called *detached buttonhole stitch*, and was used at least 6,000 years ago.

Holes are an essential part of any lace, however, and it was not until the 14th century AD that lace as we know it began. These early laces were really a form of cutwork embroidery, but in the next stage of the development of needlelace the interlocking stitches were secured to a tracing thread rather than to the cut edges of a fabric. This thread supported the work and at the same time provided an outline to the design, which might be geometric, naturalistic, stylized or abstract. Fruits and flowers appeared in abundance, also figures of kings and queens, crowns, flags, weapons and hunting scenes.

Needlelace is essentially flat, or two-dimensional. The detached buttonhole stitches are worked in rows, from right to left and from left to right.

The centres of manufacture

Needlelaces were the first laces to be used in high fashion. From the 1550s to 1625 all the nobility of Europe displayed stiffly starched ruffs or standing collars, raised off the shoulders, supported by wire and decorated with geometric cutwork or *punto in aria*. Lace manufacture became fiercely competitive, and numerous rival centres sprang up.

VENICE   In about 1650, Venice captured the market with a dramatic three-dimensional needlelace of huge stylized flowers within swollen rims, the solid areas so finely worked, in such slender linen thread, that 6,000 detached buttonhole stitches were needed to cover a space 2.5cm (1in) square. These laces were very slow to make, and extremely expensive. Their importation, with prodigal abandon, into France, England and Spain resulted in huge trade deficits.

To support the stitches of punto in aria *and its successors, a special frame was devised to replace the cut linen which had supported the stitches at the end of every row. It took the form of a double outlining thread, or tracing thread (from the French* fil de trace).

In early laces, holes were cut in woven linen and the spaces were then filled with detached buttonhole stitches. The next step was to remove the linen, leaving the interlocking stitches 'in the air'. These laces were first associated with Venice, where they were called ponto in aere *in the local dialect or, in Italian,* punto in aria. *(Courtesy of Cornell University, New York.)*

FRANCE   Fifteen years later, the techniques and designs of Venetian needlelace had been stolen by the French, who within another ten years had developed their own style, known as *point de France*. Architectural designers were hired to produce a lighter lace of imposing dignity, characterized by a disciplined precision and symmetry of construction.

Constant change was soon necessary to keep consumers happy, and different styles – Argentan, Argentella and Alençon – were successively developed. In the frivolous ambience of the early and middle years of the 18th century, the density of the lace designs was diminished, and the areas of openwork enlarged, while the decorative stitches became ever more intricate and varied.

FLANDERS   That part of the Spanish empire known as Flanders lay at the north-eastern border of France. The relationship between French and Flemish laces is difficult to untangle and the object of controversy. The ceaseless wars between the two countries, with their constantly shifting frontiers, are to some extent to blame.

Point de gaze, the only truly distinctive needlelace from the Flanders area, dates from the mid-19th century, after the creation of the kingdom of Belgium in 1831.

SEDAN   Formerly independent, this principality was annexed by France in 1642. The needlelace named after the town resembled a luxuriously effervescent point de France, with voluptuous botanical shapes filled to bursting with clusters of decorative stitches.

RESEAU VENISE   This lace is of uncertain geographical origin. The term *réseau* indicates that its openwork background is in the form of a network of small regular meshes, in contrast to the large irregular 'bars' of the earlier Venetian laces. 'Venise' associates this lace with Venice – but here the argument begins.

An engraving of 1754, by Giovanni Grevembroch, shows a punto in aria *worker. She wears leather thimbles on her left thumb and forefinger. To prevent the needle slipping from her sweaty grasp and perhaps also to push it, she wears a third thimble on her right thumb. (Courtesy of the Museo Correr, Venice.)*

Wilcke Smith's picture, worked in 1980, features the legendary Fibonacci, whose Book of Counting *was published in 1202. He is wrapped in needlelace stitches and brandishes a golden whip, its tip curled around a tiny square concealing the magic decimal* phi. *Within the curve of the whip huddle generations of rabbits, their ultra-suede bodies revealed by scalpel-slashed cuts in the amate paper ground. These creatures represent Fibonacci's insight into the geometric progression of numbers, first observed in the multiplication of a single pair of rabbits.*

Imitations

Copies of antique laces, produced in the 19th and early 20th centuries, can be distinguished from genuine originals by a stiffness of texture resulting from the use of tight mechanically-even thread; a gaucheness of composition inherent in that lack of spontaneity which characterizes imitation; fewer stitches than in the old forms, which used flax fibres, handspun until they approached the fineness of gossamer; or by the substitution of cotton for linen – a practice adopted for needlelaces only in the 1850s.

Today

Modern lacemakers are no longer restricted either by savage commercial competition or by the need to cater for the flighty fluctuations of fashion. They can, at their own pace, follow their own direction. It is hoped that this book, with its new look at the magnificent laces of the past, will inspire lacemakers to venture into hitherto uncharted territory, and will encourage them not only to copy antique examples, but also to interpret the stitches imaginatively, using all their potential for creativity.

CHAPTER 1

BASIC EQUIPMENT AND SKILLS

Materials

Needles

Sharps are needed for couching down the outlining thread, since the needle has to be pushed through both the pattern and its support. A blunt-tipped needle, either ball point or tapestry, is used for working the stitches; its rounded tip cannot accidentally split the threads.

Threads

Several thicknesses of thread are often used in one piece of lace. In the following chapter, the samples featuring each stitch are worked mainly in coton perlé (pearl cotton) no. 5, a thick thread which, on a background of contrasting colour, shows up mistakes very clearly. The threads used for the projects at the end of each section are listed in the descriptions that accompany them.

Cotton threads are available in various forms – crochet, cordonnet special, perlé, à broder, brillant, and fil à dentelles, each in varying thicknesses. The first two give a crisp firm finish, while softer effects can be achieved with coton à broder. Broder 16 and perlé 3, 5 and 8 all offer an excellent choice of colours, in DMC. Silks of increasing fineness – 30/3, 40/3, 110/3 and 130/3 – blend well together and can be lustrous and colourful, while bright rayon (art silk) machine embroidery threads provide spectacular highlights.

Snarling

Threads tend to untwist or overtwist as you work. This is inevitable because the spiralling movement of the stitches will either loosen or reinforce the twist (ply) of the thread. Overtwisting can be corrected by letting the needle hang and twirl at fairly frequent intervals; untwisting by rotating the needle to tighten the thread. The effect is less bothersome if short lengths of thread are used.

When threads are plyed during manufacture, they may be turned in either a clockwise or an anti-clockwise direction. The visible effect of this is referred to as S or Z. Crochet cotton and cordonnet special have a tight Z twist. Coton à broder and coton perlé have a looser S twist.

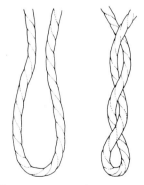

When overstrained, the balanced thread on the left overtwists, or auto-plyes, becoming snarled.

A pattern

Traditionally, lace begins as a *design*, drawn by a trained artist or draughtsman. The design shows not only the main outlines of the motifs but the appearance of the fillings to be used in each distinct area.

The design itself was kept for reference, but its outline was copied or traced, and used as the *pattern*. In the past, the pattern was mounted on parchment, and passed from one worker to another. From the 1850s, for domestic as opposed to professional lacemakers, the patterns were printed on glazed cotton, along with a series of numbers relating to the list of stitches to be used. Today, paper patterns are used, the original design being either traced or photo-copied.

A pricker

In the days when patterns were worked on parchment, holes had to be pierced to allow the needle with its couching thread to pass through. A single or double line of holes was pricked around all the contours of the design. Also, where repetition of a particular motif was important in the design, pricking through several layers at a time could ensure that all the repeats were precisely the same.

Now that patterns are made with paper and other relatively soft materials, lines of holes are unnecessary. Both pattern and support are easily penetrated by a sharp needle, and there is no problem in working the couching stitches directly along the outline. If you prefer to work with pre-made holes, you can save time by running the outline beneath the unthreaded needle of a sewing machine. The disadvantage here is that the spacing of the couching stitches is less easily varied, and the helpful flexibility – of stitches close together on a curve, further apart on the straight – is largely lost.

In the late 19th century, schools of design were set up in Ireland, and the laces were brush-drawn in Chinese white on tinted paper. This particular pattern comes from a book of designs at St Clare's Convent, Kenmare.

This French engraving dated 1676 shows a Court lady in informal dress making needlelace over a parchment pattern. (Courtesy of Antique Collectors' Club.)

Supporting and protecting the pattern

The parchment of the old patterns was stiff enough to be self-supporting; it did not crumple with handling, or pull out of shape and distort the stitches. Paper patterns, however, need some form of support, as shown. Whatever method of support is chosen, contact between lacemaker and lace will always be close, separated as they are from each other only by a short length of thread, and linked by the need for the needle to pass unerringly at every stitch through one particular loop.

In addition to being supported, the paper pattern must be protected from the constant scratching of the needle. Much the simplest shield is tinted self-adhesive acetate (contact paper), or vinyl, film. Cut the size required to cover the pattern; peel off the back; hold the film firmly, sticky side down, over the support, and static attraction will cause the pattern to leap upwards towards you. If you are nervous of misattachments – and these are quite irrevocable – first catch the pattern down to the support, using strips of two-sided adhesive tape.

Choose a tint of acetate that will contrast with the threads you intend to use. For economy, clear, matt self-adhesive book covering, available from stationers, can be substituted, in which case it is sensible to draw the pattern itself on tinted paper.

As well as protecting the pattern, the stitches must be guarded from that constant contact with the hands, most especially the left thumb, which is essential to control the tension of the thread as each stitch is made. Secretions from the hands and dirt from the air can be excluded by covering the lace with a plastic sheet cut with a central opening just large enough to expose the working area. Paper from a kitchen roll could also be used.

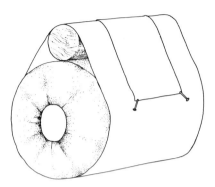

Once the paper pattern has been backed, the layers may in turn be wrapped around a firm pad, small enough to hold in the hand, or be stitched flat to an embroidery frame, or, as in the lace-making island of Burano, fixed by pins to a specially designed pillow that can rest on the knees.

Architect's linen protects the pattern as effectively as acetate film, but it has no adhesive power and must be stitched down to the support. Here, a sample of the acetate film is being peeled from its backing, ready for use. In the background, a white lace motif is shown, worked over blue-tinted acetate.

Ordinary paper is far too flexible to stand alone. The pattern could be backed with stiff brown paper, felt, or several layers of cloth. Here, a pattern drawn on tracing paper is backstitched to felt. Various types of thread and needles are also shown, as is a piece of architect's linen and, above it, some acetate film (contact paper). Either of the latter can be used to cover the pattern and attach it to the support. The pricker, in the centre, consists of a sharply-pointed pin fixed into a metal (or wood) handle.

The order of working

The success of commercial lacemaking has always depended on maximizing the perfection of the work while minimizing the time taken to complete it. Each lacemaker therefore specialized in one stage or stitch. Mme Despierres in her *History of Alençon Lace* (1887) lists the following stages in the manufacture of French needlelaces:

1   Pricking (*le picage*)
2   Laying the outline or tracing thread (*la trace*)
3   The solid design areas (*le fond* or *l'entoilage*, also called *le mat* – a flat or smooth area). The term *fond*, literally a foundation or background, is a misnomer; it was applied to the design areas of those Venetian laces, copied in France in the 17th century, in which the motifs occupied almost the entire area, with very little open space around them. As the openwork grew in extent and importance, the term *fond* should logically have been transferred to the background, but it was retained for the solid areas 'to avoid confusion'.
4   The decorative filling stitches (*le rempli*, *les jours*)
5   The ground (*les brides*, *le réseau* or in general *le champ*). Decorative grounds, especially in the form of star, circle or grid fillings were called *les modes*.
6   Superficial embellishments such as decorative raised circles or crowns (*couronnes*)
7   The raised outline (*le cordonnet*, *la relief*, *la brode*); strictly, *cordonnet* refers to the padding cords which are subsequently covered by an embroidery of buttonhole stitches.
8   The detachment of the lace from the pattern
9   Picking away the cut ends of thread
10 Repair, or making good any imperfections in the work
11 Assembling the parts and joining them together

Today's lacemakers have to cope with all the stages and all the stitches by themselves, and the inflexibility of the past no longer serves any useful purpose. For any sizeable piece, it is easier to begin in the middle, regardless of the kind of stitch which fills that area.

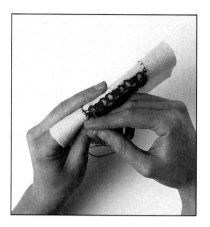

A method described for the Zele (Belgian) lace of today, recommends laying the pattern over the left forefinger while holding it firmly between the thumb and ring finger. The thread is then supported beneath the middle finger, while the needle is held 'like a cigarette' in the right hand, and pushed through with the thimbled thumb.

Facing page: Parts of a lace

ground

mode

cordonnet

filling

solid design areas

fillings

mode

heading

Laying the outline

A firm outline of thread is essential for all needlelaces, both to define the shape of the design and to provide an anchorage for the rows of stitches which will pass forwards and back between them. In French, this thread is called *la trace*, a literal translation of which is tracing, and in English, *tracing thread* can conveniently be used. Alternative terms are contour thread, outlining thread and foundation cord. The abbreviation tt is used here.

The tt is secured tightly to the pattern by horizontal couching stitches worked along the drawn outline. The couching threads are

1 Tts may also outline the enclosures containing different rempli. Separate the two strands of the tt and couch one around the enclosure until it joins up again with the double strand. Remember to interlock the tts at every junction so that they cannot separate when the couching stitches are removed. Here, the pattern is held to the felt by self-adhesive transparent shelving film.

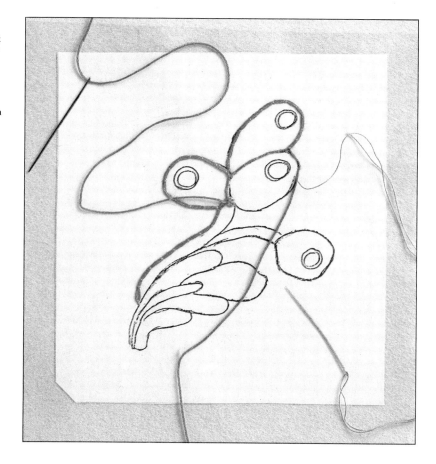

the only ones to pass through the pattern; all other threads rest on top. You must never forget that once the lace is off the pattern, only the continuity of the tt and the unfailing attachment of stitch rows to it, will prevent the whole thing falling apart.

It is a wise precaution to make the tt at least twice as long as the actual outline by taking it all around and back again. Double the thread over, and use the loop as the starting point, since this will be easy to secure. If you have a highly convoluted outline, the length needed will be difficult to assess. If the thread runs out, a new one can be joined on by buttonholing the overlapped ends tightly together with the couching thread. Alternatively, they can simply be run through the couching stitches, in either direction.

It is usual to match the colour of the tt with the sewing thread. In some of the worked samples, a lighter colour has been used to show the method of attachment. It may also be advantageous for the colour of the couching thread to match that of the lace.

The tt must be quite taut or it will sag as the rows of stitches pull against it. Secure it beneath the left thumb as you make each couching stitch, to prevent slippage. At sharp angles, the couching thread may be knotted tightly at the back of the work.

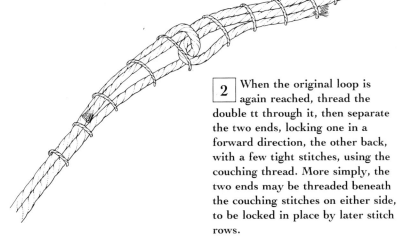

2 When the original loop is again reached, thread the double tt through it, then separate the two ends, locking one in a forward direction, the other back, with a few tight stitches, using the couching thread. More simply, the two ends may be threaded beneath the couching stitches on either side, to be locked in place by later stitch rows.

The direction of working

Traditionally, French and Belgian needlelaces were worked *face side up*. The stitches pass from *left to right*, with the needle pointing away. For the most part, the *return threads* (right–left rows) have no stitches, but are carried either straight back or whipped around the loops of the previous row. It was rare in 18th-century laces for stitches to be worked in both directions, but the technique became more common in 19th-century laces, such as point de gaze.

The direction in which an antique lace was worked – with the needle pointing towards or away from the worker – can be determined from the direction of loop closure. As the detached buttonhole stitch is made, the threads must cross over to close the loop in either an **S** or **Z** direction. The acuteness of the snarling effect depends not only on the tightness and direction (S or Z) of the original spin, but also on the tightness of the ply, and the amount of convolution involved in the stitch formation.

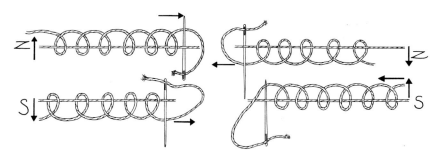

In all French and Belgian needlelaces, the cross, or loop closure, is in a *Z-direction* (like the middle stroke of a letter Z). Z-closures are produced either by working the stitches L–R with the needle pointing away, or by working the stitches R–L with the needle pointing towards the worker. There is documentary evidence that in antique French laces the first method was used. An *S-direction* crossover, found in some Venetian and Youghal laces, is produced by working L–R with the needle pointing towards, or R–L with the needle pointing away from the worker.

The solid design areas

These are the densest areas of the design. The stitch used for them is the same in all French and Belgian needlelaces: the *detached buttonhole stitch (dbs) with a straight return*.

As each loop is closed, the thread crosses over in a **Z** direction. The anchorage at the tt is important, not only to hold the completed row at the correct tension, but also to bring the sewing thread to the required height for the next row. Several twists may be needed. It is usually best to take the sewing thread under the tt, and then back over.

The rows of stitches are normally worked lengthwise across the area, gracefully following the curvature of the outline. Additional part-rows will be added as necessary.

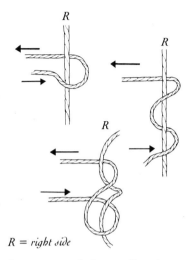

R = right side

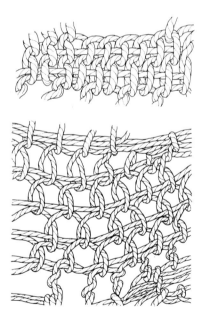

Dbs with a straight return has two forms: *close*, in which the stitches are packed very tightly together, with up to 30 per cm (½in), or *open* in which they are spaced more widely apart. The close form is found in all French and Venetian needlelaces; the open form is characteristic only of the Belgian needlelace known as point de gaze.

Loops are made in one direction only: they pass across the enclosure to the far side, where the thread is wrapped around the tt and carried straight back. The drawing shows variations taken from the antique lace.

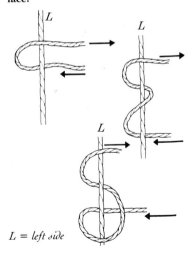

L = left side

Working samples

The direction of working described earlier has been followed here.

To practise the stitches, no elaborate set-up is needed. Using a water-soluble marker, rule out the sides of an enclosure approximately 7.5cm (3in) square, or smaller if finer thread is used. No drawn pattern is needed for the simpler stitches, and the tt can be couched directly to the fabric, which should be sufficiently smooth and firm to prevent its threads being caught up by the needle and to ensure that it does not crumple with constant handling. For more complex stitches, where a pattern is used, a covering of acetate film will give additional support.

When you have stitched your sample, finish by securing the sewing thread to the tt by running it through the couching stitches. In the samples, the enclosures can be left open at the top.

In working projects, as opposed to samples, the shapes allocated to different stitches are unlikely to be straight-sided, and you may need to add stitches at the sides or part-rows at intervals, in order to fill the area neatly. It is essential, when modifications of this kind are made, that the general rhythm of the stitch formation is not disturbed.

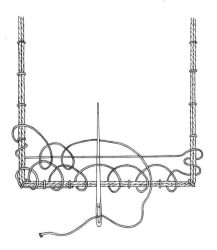

Beginning at the lower L corner:
Row 1 **Attach the sewing thread to the tt by a small knot, or run it through the couching stitches. Work a row of dbs over the lower tt, making them all the same size, evenly distanced and fairly close together.**
Row 2 **After coiling the thread around the R-hand tt, return it straight back to the L. The straight return threads act as stabilizers, preventing the loops from being pulled out of shape as the stitches of the following row pass through them.**

Row 3 **Each stitch of the second loop row will take in a loop from row 1 plus a portion of the row 2 return thread.**
Repeat rows 2 and 3 until the area is filled.

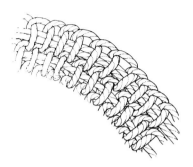

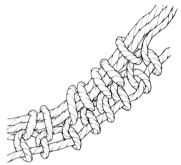

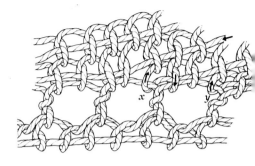

At the top, the last row of stitches may be worked directly over the tt. Alternatively, the stitch row can be

completed and then the return thread used to whip the loops and the tt securely together.

Here, a part-row has been worked to fill out the shape. At X and Y, the return thread curves back on itself to start a new row of stitches.

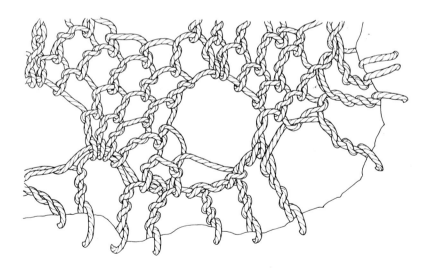

In flat laces, to relieve the congested effect, the filling stitch enclosures are often lined with wide loops, and the rows begin and end over these, rather than over a tt already cluttered with dbs stitches.

Loose ends

It is difficult to make a neat join in the middle of a row, and the length of thread remaining in the needle should be assessed before each new row is begun so that all ends can be left and new threads started at the perimeter. The ends can either be knotted at that point, or passed beneath the couching stitches and sewn in more firmly later, or covered by the stitches of the solid design areas. Leave about 12mm (½in) beyond the run-in, to prevent the thread being accidentally pulled through.

In raised laces, any messiness at the tt will be concealed beneath the padded cordonnet. The various ends will themselves have the effect of padding, reducing the need for additional strands.

In flat or partially flat laces, such as point de France, point de Sedan and réseau Venise, concealment is much more difficult. A neater cover-up of the outline can be made by working the dbs after the rempli, using the close stitching of the final row to take in any loose ends. Alternatively, a scarcely visible overcasting will produce a neat finish.

The use of a continuous line of buttonholing to cover every junction-line derives from 18th-century French needlelaces, and may look clumsy in other styles. If necessary, ends can be taken through to the reverse side of the work and run in later, but be careful that these ends are not cut through with the couching stitches when the lace is detached from its support.

Correcting mistakes

Mistakes will happen, but be vigilant and try to spot them at the time; the forced unpicking of several rows can be exquisitely tedious. To unpick, the needle can either be taken back through the stitch movements, or it can be unthreaded and the thread pulled through. This is quicker, but it can all too easily tug on the stitches, distorting those you need to preserve.

If the mistake is not too conspicuous, it may be better to leave it; unpicking weakens the thread. If the area is a total disaster it can be cut out by severing its attachment to the tt or to the lining loops.

The decorative fillings

Many of the filling stitches look complicated, but a surprising number are simplicity itself when broken down into stages. Getting the tension right can be the most difficult part.

Except for point de gaze, the majority of the filling stitches in French and Flemish needlelaces are worked in *twisted buttonhole stitch*. Essentially, this is dbs with an additional twist in the side of the loop.

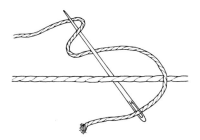

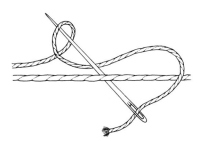

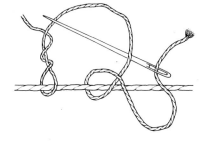

There are three ways in which the additional twist can be inserted. The first is by corkscrewing the needle through the thread.

The second is by making a loop with the fingers, or around a finger, then taking the needle through the loop.

The third is by working a dbs, pulling the thread through until the loop is the size required, then holding the loop in position with the left thumb and taking the needle back under the thread.

The twisted buttonhole stitch (tbs), occurs in an immense variety of stitch formations, being grouped into 2s, 3s, 4s, 5s and 6s. The groups are sometimes so tightly packed together that they appear as dense clusters, and the thread course is difficult to follow.

There may be large loops between them, so strongly arched that the sequence of stitch rows becomes obscure, or the clusters may be staggered from one row to the next, creating zigzags, or solid and open diamonds of intricate formation.

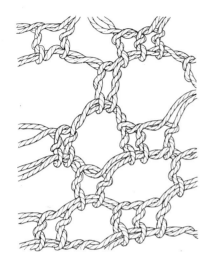

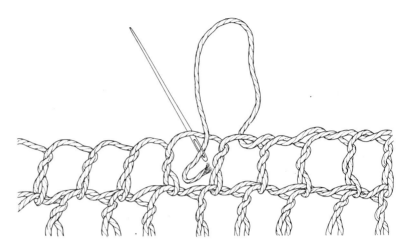

The tbs has two forms. In the extended version the thread is left slightly slack and the twists are clearly visible.

In the contracted or compressed version, the second twist is forced down on the first, so that it bulges out with the pressure until it looks like a knot. In its extreme form the contracted tbs is known as *hollie stitch*.

The return thread, passing from right to left, is no longer straight, but whips or curls its way in and out of the loops in a snaky fashion.

It may pass through every loop of the previous row, or only occasional ones, the choice depending on which method is sufficient to hold it in place.

During working, the large loops between the clusters may, if necessary, be held out with insect pins, or clipped in position with a couching stitch, or the loops may be taken over a guide thread run across the area to keep the heights even.

In the late 17th and early 18th centuries, the decorative fillings became ever more numerous, elaborate and fanciful, yet they are still nothing but variations on a theme, and you will find that they are far less difficult than may appear at first sight.

The decorative fillings of different needlelaces are an aid to their identification, and will be described in the separate sections.

The embellishments, the relief and the ground

Traditionally, the ground is worked after the fillings and before the raised work. The style of ground, which varies in the different laces, is an aid to their identification, and so will be described individually for each type. Embellishments include padded rings and various forms of picot. These also vary in different laces and will be discussed under their heads.

The relief refers to the raised outlines of the motifs, which make the lace three-dimensional. A variable number of padding strands are laid over the tt in the required position, and are covered with buttonhole stitches which catch them down to the lace. Such stitches are passed through a pre-existing fabric, and so are a form of

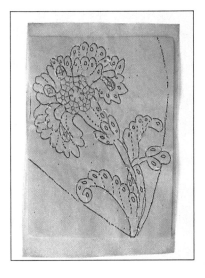

Once the lace is completed, the couching stitches that hold down the tt can be cut. This reverse side of the Argentella project shows the appearance of the stitches before cutting begins.

If the pattern has been supported on two or three layers of cloth, it may be easier to cut between the layers to get at the stitches. Here, they are cut with a scalpel between the paper pattern and the felt backing.

As soon as all the couching stitches are cut, the lace can be lifted off, exposing the original set-up of pattern covered by tinted film, which can now be used again.

The assembly

Large items, such as a long deep flounce, could only be completed in a reasonable time by sharing the work out among many lacemakers. The repeats would be divided between groups and, when finished, the pieces would be invisibly joined, either by taking the stitches along the tt of a motif, or by working additional stitches to link parts of the ground.

embroidery. An alternative name for the relief is therefore *la brode* (embroidery). In former days, it would have been carried out by a *brodeuse* (embroiderer).

Yet another name for the raised outline is the *cordonnet*, a term in existence at least since the mid-18th century. The brode or cordonnet may form a thin, ridged rim, emphasizing the contours of the motifs like a dark outline; or it may occur in restricted areas, highlighting an otherwise flat lace, as in point de France or point de Sedan.

The cordonnet also has a more practical function: it gives an opportunity for irregularities of outline to be corrected, for ends of threads to be gathered in and concealed, and for weaknesses of attachment to be strengthened.

The threads used for buttonholing over the cordonnet are customarily thicker than the sewing thread, but the precise form taken by the cordonnet itself will be described under the different laces.

Finishing

Any cut fragments of couching thread clinging to the lace must be picked away, with tweezers if necessary. If they have been impaled on the sewing threads they may be impossible to remove. This demonstrates the advantage of using the same colour for both couching and needlelace stitches.

Once the lace is set free, minor defects or loose ends may become apparent. In commercial laces, this stage was a most important one, providing a very elaborate cover-up operation to improve the quality of the finished product.

CHAPTER 2

STITCHES FROM TRADITIONAL LACES

Seven antique laces from France and Belgium are described in this chapter. Between them they cover a span of 250 years.

A photograph of each, approximately actual size, is accompanied by a brief historical introduction which pinpoints the differences between their decorative stitches and other embellishments. Individual stitch formations from the antique lace are then drawn, and instructions for working them are illustrated by samples and in some cases by additional stitch diagrams.

The formations have been numbered rather than named, for the excellent reason that to date no consistent terminology exists. Irrelevant geographical references, expressed in French – such as point de Turque, point d'Espagne, point d'Anvers, point de Grecques, and point de Bruxelles – go along with a plurality of names for each stitch, and a plurality of stitches for each name. They are relics from the practical needlework magazines popular before World War I, and are long overdue for revision. Readers who already have favourite names for particular stitches can write them in at the appropriate places.

Each section ends with a project, based on designs and stitches from the antique lace. The project can be worked as it is shown, or alternatively it may inspire ideas for creating your own traditional or quasi-traditional patterns, using the stitches you like best. The progression from square to multiform projects may seem intimidating, but it is really only the size and shape of the enclosures which change. Each area is simply a space, outlined by a tt, and waiting to be filled with stitches.

The following abbreviations have been used:

dbs	detached buttonhole stitch
L	left
R	right
sr(s)	straight return(s)
st(s)	stitch(es)
tbs	twisted buttonhole stitch
tt	tracing thread

In the diagrams, the numbers indicate the number of stitches in a group; the dashes indicate gaps bridged by a loop, '–' representing a short gap, and '– –' a longer loop.

In the standing collars and cuffs, each geometric shape is supported by a frame of warps and wefts left in the cut linen. Though the same stitches are used throughout, the first technique is embroidery, the second needlelace. From this punto in aria developed all the later French and Belgian needlelaces. (Robert Peake, c1620; courtesy of Sotheby Parke Bernet and Co., London.)

POINT DE FRANCE

About 1650, Venice captured the market with a magnificent three-dimensional lace of huge flowers with padded rims, made with such fine thread that 6,000 of its buttonhole stitches occupied a space only 2.5cm (1in) square. Understandably, it was very slow to work, and so immensely expensive that France and England were almost bankrupted by its prodigal importation.

Fifteen years later, the devious and unscrupulous manoeuvres of Louis XIV and his finance minister Colbert had brought Venetian lacemakers to France. From them, French needlewomen, established at the royal factories of Alençon, Argentan and Sedan, soon learned the techniques and stitches of Venetian lace.

Within another ten years, France had adapted the lace to its own temperament, and *point de France* was created. Architect-designers were appointed to produce a lace of imposing dignity, in which small motifs – of suns, crowns, pavilions, eastern figurines and symbols of war – were set with disciplined precision and symmetry into a background of large hexagonal meshes, buttonholed over and spiked with Venetian picots.

The solid design areas consisted of closely worked dbs with a straight return, lightened by openings known as *portes*, arranged either singly or in groups of four, known as *quadrilles*. The rows of stitches were worked lengthwise of each motif, following its curves.

The decorative fillings consisted mainly of groupings of stitches into 3s, 4s, 5s or 6s so that they looked like tiny bricks in a wall of pierced construction.

The lace was mainly flat, with relief used only to give emphasis to selected areas. The raised outlines were only slightly tapered, and padded crowns haloed with loops were implanted at the centres of flowers.

Detail of a collar intended to pass smoothly around the shoulders, c1700

POINT DE FRANCE 1

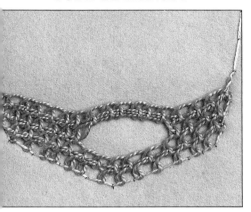

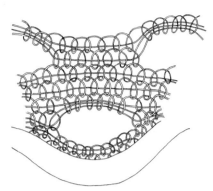

POINT DE FRANCE 2

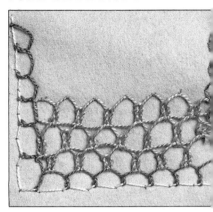

The solid design areas are worked in dbs with an sr. The small openings are called *portes*. They may appear singly or in larger groupings.

Rows 1 to 3 Work two rows of dbs, with an sr thread between them.
Row 4 At the beginning of the porte, lift the return thread in an arched loop passing over several sts of row 3. Continue in dbs to the end. To prevent the loop collapsing, it may be held out with a pin, or the return thread may be taken through the loop on either side.

Row 5 Work dbs to the beginning of the arched loop. Carry the thread parallel to that of row 4, then continue buttonholing to the R side.
Row 6 Carry the return thread back to the L side, arching it parallel to rows 4 and 5.
Row 7 Work dbs right across, closing the top of the porte with 6 sts. Each closing st must take in the loop threads of rows 4, 5 and 6.

Lining loops Work a single row of contracted tbs, spaced apart, to line the inside of the tt. Go around again, whipping the thread through each loop, entering below and exiting above, in other words with the needle pointed away.

The sample Beginning at the bottom L corner:
Row 1 Work a pair of tbs in the middle of each of the lining loops, linking the pairs by arched loops held out by pins, or supported by the left thumb nail. At the R side, pass the thread around a lining loop before turning back.

POINT DE FRANCE 3

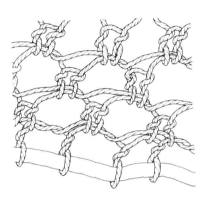

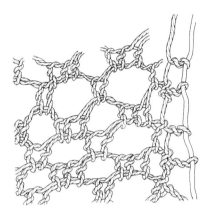

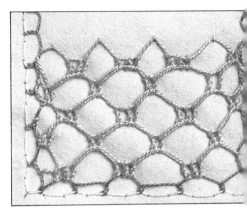

Row 2 Whip the return thread once around each longer loop but not around the short loops. The return thread will have almost the appearance of a straight line. At the L side, pass the thread around a lining loop.

Row 3 Work a pair of tbs into each long loop of row 1, taking in the thread of row 2. Leave long loops between these pairs.

Row 4 Repeat row 2.

Continue in this way until the space is filled. Make sure that the rhythm of the st pattern is maintained.

The tbs are more extended than in point de France 2. The lining of loops has no whipped return. The general arrangement of the decorative sts is:

Rows
5		3	3	3	3	3
3			2	2	2	2	2
1		3	3	3	3	3

Row 1 Beginning at the lower L corner, work 3 tbs close together in the first lining loop. °Leave an arched loop. Work 3 tbs. Continue from ° to the R side and pass the thread around the nearest lining loop.

Row 2 Whip the return thread once around every loop. At the L side take the needle twice under and over a lining loop.

Row 3 Work a pair of tbs into each long loop of row 1. Leave arched loops over each 3-st group.

Row 4 As row 2.

Repeat these four rows until the space is filled.

Point de France 3 can be worked either widthwise or lengthwise in relation to the space.

POINT DE FRANCE 4

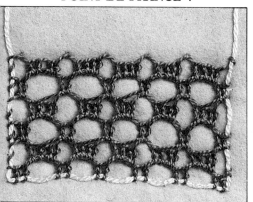

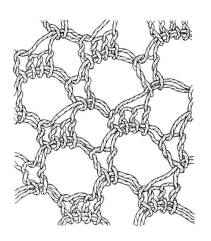

POINT DE FRANCE 5

Work as in point de France 3, but substituting 4 sts for every group of 3.

Rows					
5	4	4	4	4	4
3		2	2	2	2
1	4	4	4	4	4

Work as point de France 3, but substituting 5 sts for every 3. The loops between the groups are less strongly arched. The return thread is carried straight over the longer loops, but whipped under and over the smaller loops within the groups.

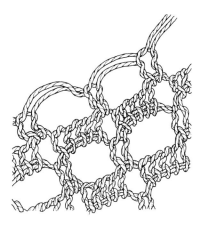

POINT DE FRANCE 6

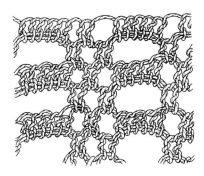

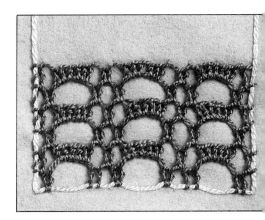

Rows

5	5	5	5	5	5
3		2	2	2	2
1	5	5	5	5	5

Rows

```
7 1 1 1 1 1 - - 1 1 - - 1 1 1 1 1 1 - - 1 1 - -
5 - - - - - 1 1 - - 1 1 - - - - - - 1 1 - - 1 1
3 1 1 1 1 1 - - 1 1 - - 1 1 1 1 1 1 - - 1 1 - -
1 - - - - - 1 1 - - 1 1 - - - - - - 1 1 - - 1 1
```

The stitch is contracted tbs. The formation is basically similar to point de France 4 and 5. There are lining loops in the larger enclosures, but not in the smaller ones.

The st rows alternate with return rows 2, 4, 6 and 8.

Row 1 Beginning at the lower L corner, anchor the sewing thread to the tt. Leave a long arched loop. °Work 2 tbs, leave a loop the width of 2 sts. Repeat from ° to the end.

Row 2 The return thread passes parallel to the long loops and is whipped around the narrow loops between sts.

Row 3 Work 6 tbs into each long loop, and 2 into the short loops. Repeat to end.

Row 4 As row 2.

Repeat rows 3 and 4 until the space is filled.

POINT DE FRANCE 7

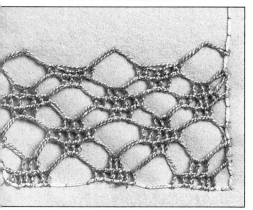
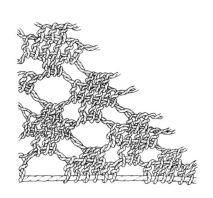

POINT DE FRANCE 8 A vein

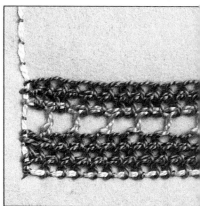

Rows

```
9 1 1 1 1 1 1 - - - - 1 1 1 1 1 1 - - - - 1 1 1 1 1 1 - - -
7 - 1 1 1 - - 1 1 1 - - 1 1 1 - - 1 1 1 - - 1 1 1 - - - -
5 1 - - - - 1 1 1 1 1 1 - - - - 1 1 1 1 1 1 - - - - 1 1 1 1
3 - 1 1 1 - - 1 1 1 - - 1 1 1 - - 1 1 1 - - 1 1 1 - - 1 1 1
1 1 1 1 1 1 1 - - - - 1 1 1 1 1 1 - - - - 1 1 1 1 1 1 - - -
```

There are no lining loops, and the contracted tbs are hung directly over the tt.

Rows of sts grouped in 3s alternate with rows of sts grouped in 6s.

The return thread rows (2, 4, 6 and so on) whip over some of the shorter loops, and once over each long loop. The effect is of small solid diamond shapes, separated by diagonal lines of holes. A variation of this stitch (not illustrated) has rows of 3s alternating with rows of 8s.

Work 5 rows of dbs with an sr. Ending at the R side, leave this thread, and rejoin at the L side. Work one row of tbs. Make an sr, and then continue in dbs as before.

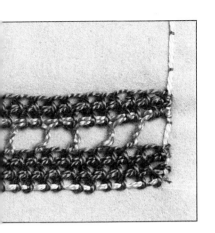

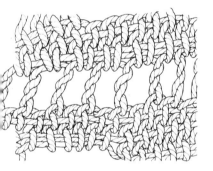

POINT DE FRANCE 9

The stitch used is contracted tbs. It is worked lengthwise of the area that it fills. There are no lining loops. In the 17th-century lace, the width of each completed diamond was 3mm (⅛in).

The return thread (even) rows are not whipped through every loop, but only sufficiently to keep the holes clear. Each 12 rows forms one complete pattern.

Beginning at the lower L corner, work as shown in the diagram. The drawing, and the photograph of a sample worked in coton perlé 5, indicate the st spacing and loop lengths. Hold the loops out with pins if necessary.

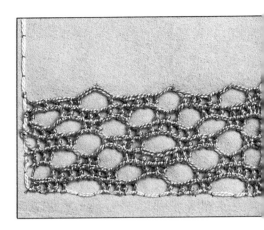

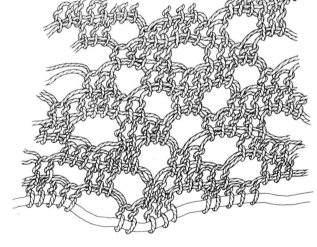

Rows

```
13  1 1 1 1 1 - - - 1 1 1 1 1 - - 1 1 1 1 1 - - - 1 1 1 1 1
11   - - 1 1 1 1 1 1 1 1 1 - - 1 1 1 - - 1 1 1 1 1 1 1 1 1 - -
 9  1 1 1 - - 1 1 1 - - 1 1 1 1 1 1 1 1 1 - - 1 1 1 - - 1 1 1
 7   1 1 1 1 1 - - 1 1 1 1 1 - - - 1 1 1 1 1 - - 1 1 1 1 1 -
 5  1 1 1 - - 1 1 1 - - 1 1 1 1 1 1 1 1 1 - - 1 1 1 - - 1 1 1
 3   - - 1 1 1 1 1 1 1 1 1 - - 1 1 1 - - 1 1 1 1 1 1 1 1 1 - -
 1  1 1 1 1 1 - - - 1 1 1 1 1 - - 1 1 1 1 1 - - - 1 1 1 1 1
```

POINT DE FRANCE 10 A linking stitch

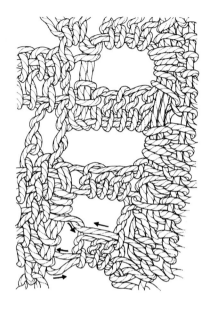

This links two areas of dbs worked at right angles to each other.

Area 1 This is worked horizontally. At the R side the thread is taken around a tt.

Area 2 This is worked vertically. The final row is whipped to a tt. Both sides of the open channel are therefore lined by tt. The tbs links pass across the space like the rungs of a ladder. The method of working is shown in the drawing.

POINT DE FRANCE 11 The ground (*champ*)

This is formed of approximately hexagonal meshes of bars in which every side is covered with buttonhole stitches. In the antique lace, each mesh side measures 2mm (¹⁄₁₂in) and bears 16 to 20 sts. Every side of every mesh has one or two Venetian picots, facing either inwards or outwards. This type of ground developed in the 1670s, as the elements of the lace design became smaller and needed to be held together more securely. A finer thread was used for it than for either the solid design areas or the filling stitches. The buttonholing of the outline is a sequence intended to cover every side without duplication.

To practise the stitch, copy the pattern illustrated, and couch a double tt along the outer border. Make a small hoop of couching thread at every mesh corner. Attach the sewing thread at A by a small knot. Make a loop to B, passing beneath the hoops at M, L and C, and over the tt. Buttonhole closely from B to C, working one or two Venetian picots along the way. Loop from C to D, passing beneath hoop E.
Buttonhole D to E. Loop E to F.
Buttonhole F to G. Loop G to H.
Buttonhole from H – I – J – G – K – E – C – L – M to A.
Make a tight knot at A.
Whip the thread down to N, and continue to make meshes as before. The thread is quite likely to run out in the middle of the work, but the

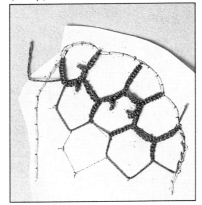

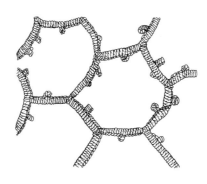

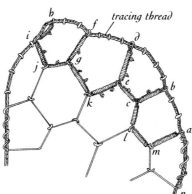

tracing thread

whip stitch

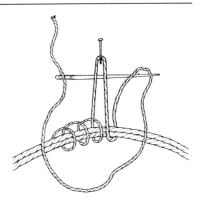

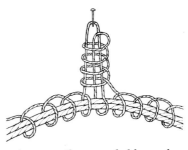

ends are easily concealed beneath the next sts.

Venetian picot At the required point, carry the thread up into a tall loop and pin it in position. Pass the thread beneath the tt and up again. Insert the needle from L to R under the first 3 threads and over the fourth, making a tight buttonhole st immediately below the pin. Make a series of buttonhole sts below this until the tt is reached. Continue buttonholing to the next picot.

POINT DE FRANCE 12 The crowns

These and the *cordonnet* (stitch 13) are added when the rest of the work is complete. The crowns, or *couronnes*, are sometimes decorated with ring picots or with inwardly-directed Venetian picots (this last variation is not shown here).

The crowns These are bulging circles like mini-doughnuts. In the antique lace they are only 2.5mm (¹⁄₁₀in) across, or 4.25mm (¹⁄₆in) including the picots. Small simple crowns are called *rings*. They can be made in various ways:

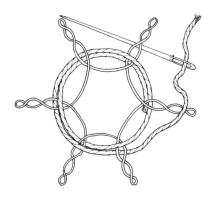
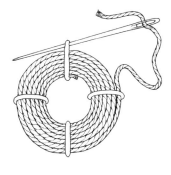
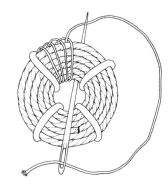

Method 1 Weave the sewing thread in and out of the surrounding sts until a padded circle is formed.

Method 2 Make hoops of couching threads on the actual lace and run the padding strands through them until the circle is sufficiently plump.

Method 3 The hoops of couching thread can alternatively be made separately on the support cloth. When the ring is completed, release it, and stab-stitch it to the lace.

Method 4 Wind the padding strand several times around a circular support of the required size, such as a knitting needle or a ring stick. The latter gives a choice of diameters. Whip around the padding to hold it together, then buttonhole over it. As the last st is completed, pass the needle through the back of the first st to close the ring. Ease the ring off the stick, and stab-stitch it to the lace.

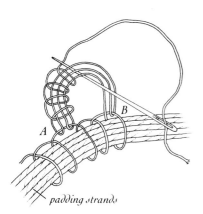

padding strands

Ring picots The ring picots look like near-circular hoops, sprouting from the outer borders of the crowns. The antique lace has up to 10 ring picots per crown. These must be worked during the buttonholing. To make a ring picot, at the required point, take the thread back over 2 sts to make a rounded loop. Pass it through the top of st A, back to B, and back again to A. Buttonhole over this treble thread, pointing the needle outwards. Continue to buttonhole over the crown until the point for the next ring picot is reached.

POINT DE FRANCE 13 The cordonnet

In addition to the crowns, relief is provided by the *cordonnet*, which is added like a heavy outline to highlight in a sensitive and artistic manner restricted areas of this otherwise flat lace. This outline may be of uniform diameter or it may swell and taper in a restrained manner. The term refers strictly to the padding strands, of variable number, that are laid over the tt and subsequently fastened to it, to give a raised effect. In the antique lace the cordonnet had 50 sts per cm (½in).

To achieve the tapered effect, make a series of couching loops along either side of the line to be raised, placing them wider apart in the middle and closer together at the end. Using soft stranded cotton, which will cling together, cut it into graduated lengths, shorter in the central area to make it bulge more. Lay these strands over the tt, cover them with a long strand to give a smooth contour, then whip over all the padding, taking the thread through the loops on either side to secure it firmly. Buttonhole closely over it, working tight Venetian picots along the outer border as you go (see point de France 11). A shallower form of cordonnet is shown in the worked sample.

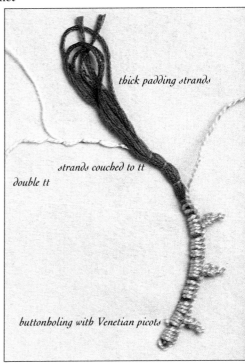

thick padding strands

strands couched to tt

double tt

buttonholing with Venetian picots

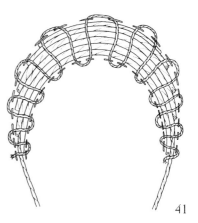

Stained glass

In this project, the various enclosures have been filled with stitches different from those in the 17th-century lace. Coloured silks have been used instead of monochrome linen thread. The flat borders, without a cordonnet, have been invisibly oversewn or buttonholed to conceal any loose ends of thread. The stitch rows follow the long axis of the area, accentuating the curves.

Threads

The threads used were as follows: solid design areas, 40/3 silk; filling stitches, 100/3 silk; cordonnet, coton perlé 8; ground, silver machine embroidery thread.

Worked by Olwyn Scott, Stained Glass *is designed to be hung between two sheets of clear acrylic, sufficiently spaced apart to avoid pressure, and then clipped together. The design is based on a single motif, measuring 3.9 × 3.3 cm (1.6 × 1.3 in), from the 17th-century collar. An encircling band has been added to support the projections. The numbers refer to the stitches used.*

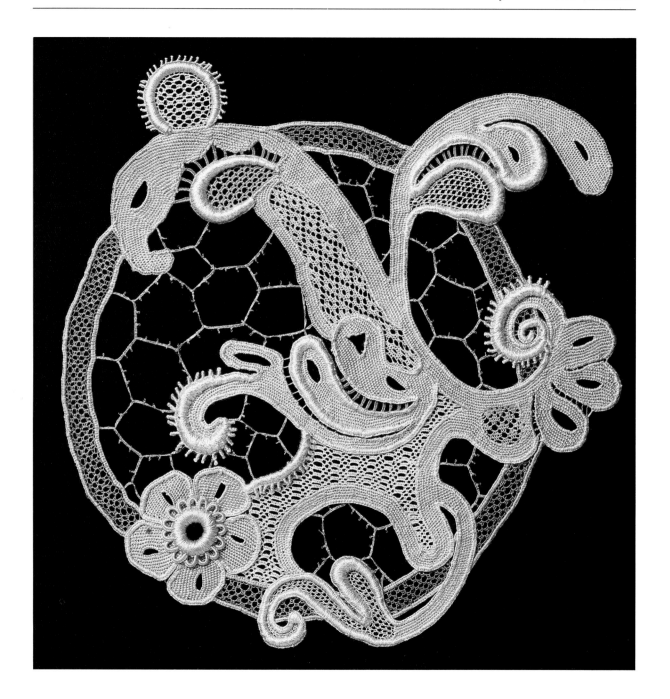

POINT DE SEDAN

The principality of Sedan, formerly independent, became part of the royal domain of France in 1642. In 1665, a lacemaking centre was established there, at the same time as the Normandy centres around Alençon, where point de France was produced.

In Sedan, the Venetian influence was less strong. The town lay on the chronically disputed and constantly shifting frontier between France and Flanders, where battles raged almost ceaselessly throughout Louis XIV's long reign (1643–1715). The influence of Flanders upon its lace must therefore have been almost as strong as that of France, and point de Sedan is sometimes regarded as a Flemish lace.

Point de Sedan resembles point de France in the large meshwork of its ground, and openwork again occupies relatively little space. But point de Sedan is flatter, with very little relief. The decorative areas, though larger, are again lined with loops. The stitches are worked in tbs, and many are similar in their groupings, though the

The sketch shows varied directions of working for a single stitch formation.

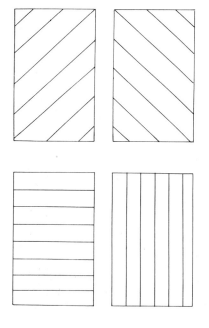

44

high curvature of the arched loops and the varied directions of the rows may make them appear unfamiliar. A new development is the very tight crowding of the groups of stitches to form clusters.

Point de Sedan differs particularly in its design, where a riot of voluptuous botanical shapes, filled to bursting with extravagant rempli, sprawl across the field. Their breath-taking variety is to some extent an illusion. Different directions of the same stitch formations – widthwise, lengthwise, diagonally right or diagonally left – produce totally different effects, and only close study reveals that the actual stitch movements are the same.

The strict emphasis on symmetry has gone. Rigidity has been replaced by a gently controlled rotundity, tinged with an eastern opulence beloved of Europe in the late 17th and early 18th centuries. Nevertheless, the crowded shapes of the stylized petals, the vigorously curving fronds, and the fretwork of portes piercing the solid areas of design with light, show links not only with point de France, but with the later development of the Normandy laces which now bear the names Argentan, Argentella and Alençon.

Detail of a sleeve ruffle, c1700

POINT DE SEDAN 1

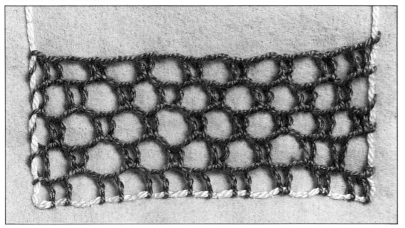

POINT DE SEDAN 2

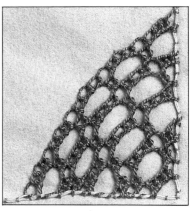

This is similar to point de France 2, but the return thread is whipped through the short loops instead of passing straight above them. It may be worked diagonally of the space, or straight on. The stitches are grouped in pairs, which alternate in successive stitch rows, and large loops arch upwards between the pairs.

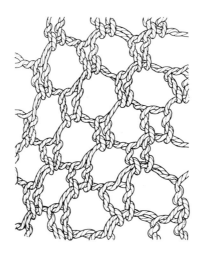

```
2  2  2  2  2  2  2
   2  2  2  2  2  2
2  2  2  2  2  2  2
   2  2  2  2  2  2
```

The stitch used is contracted tbs with a whipped return.
In point de France, this stitch is worked with shallow loops, in horizontal rows. In point de Sedan, it may alternatively be arranged in diagonal rows with tall loops.

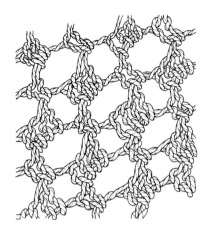

Rows

7	–	4	–	4	–	4	–	4
5	2	–	2	–	2	–	2	–
3	–	4	–	4	–	4	–	4
1	2	–	2	–	2	–	2	–

POINT DE SEDAN 3

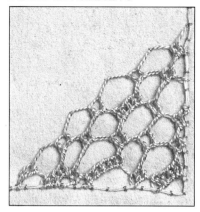

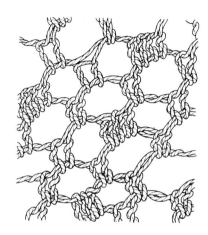

Rows

7	1 1	-----	cluster	-----	1 1	-----	cluster
5	-----	1 1	-----	1 1	-----	1 1	-----
3	cluster	-----	1 1	-----	cluster	-----	1 1
1	-----	1 1	-----	1 1	-----	1 1	-----

Line the enclosure with a single
layer of whipped loops. The pairs
of stitches in rows 1, 3, 5 and 7 are
extended to give additional height
to the strongly arched loops
between them.
These four rows make the pattern.
They are slanted diagonally. In
point de France 5, a similar
grouping is arranged horizontally.

POINT DE SEDAN 4

The stitch arrangement is one of the forms of peastitch, or *petit mignon*. The continuous rows of stitches (1, 5, 9 and so on) are worked in finer thread than the interrupted rows (3, 7, 11). The basic stitch is contracted tbs.

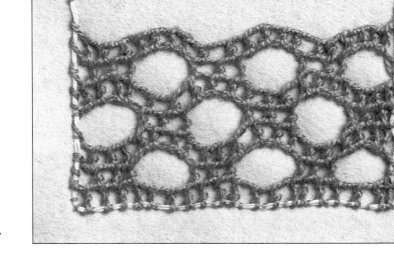

Line the area with whipped loops.
Rows 1, 5, 9 etc   Work right across.
Rows 3, 7 etc   Work 4, °take an arched loop over the next 4, work 4. Repeat from ° to the end.
The holes of row 7 alternate with those of row 3.
Rows 2, 4, 6 etc   These are R–L whipped returns.

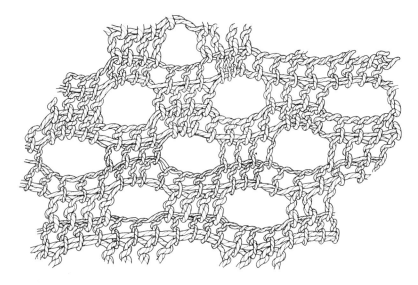

POINT DE SEDAN 5

Line the enclosure with a single row of whipped loops. The basic stitch is extended tbs with a whipped return, and 8 rows make the pattern.

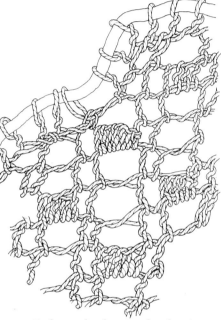

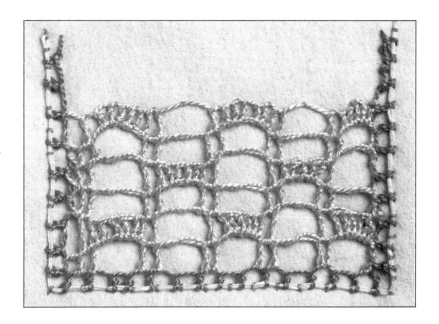

Refer to the drawing for the size and spacing of the loops. The dense clusters of 6 appear like small bricks linked by a tracery of threads.

Rows

```
9  1 1 ----- 1 1 ----- 1 1 ----- 1 1 ----- 1 1 ----- 1 1
7  1     6     1 ------- 1     6     1 ------- 1     6     1
5  1 1 ----- 1 1 ----- 1 1 ----- 1 1 ----- 1 1 ----- 1 1
3  1 ------- 1     6     1 ------- 1     6     1 ------- 1
1  1 1 ----- 1 1 ----- 1 1 ----- 1 1 ----- 1 1 ----- 1 1
```

Child's collar

The stitch rows of the decorative areas can be slanted diagonally, horizontally or vertically. The flat perimeters of the enclosures are invisibly tidied as in point de France, though it was found necessary to use a heavier support around the outside of the collar to keep it firm. The frond areas are enhanced by a raised cordonnet fixed by more obvious buttonholing.

Threads

The threads used were as follows: solid design areas and cordonnet, 40/3 silk; filling stitches, 100/3 silk.

with 3 st in alternate rows instead of 4

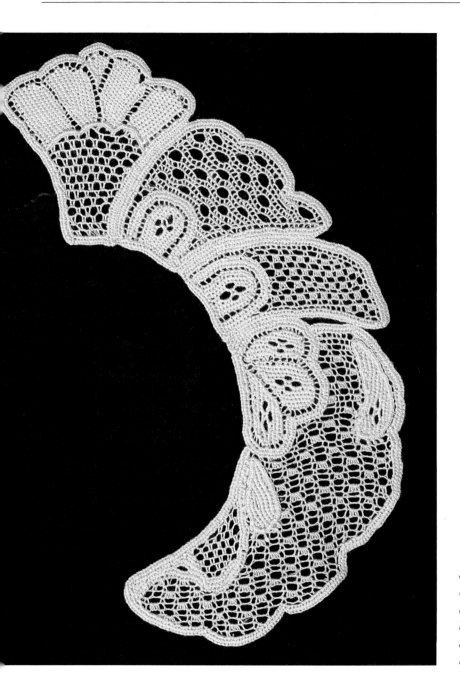

Worked by Sheila Ashby, only half of this child's collar is shown here. Simple frond shapes from the antique lace decorate the points of a design intended to show a selection of decorative stitches found in point de Sedan.

ARGENTAN

In the 18th century, the needlelaces from Normandy were grouped together under one name, *point d'Alençon* (Alençon lace). Through the decades, all retained a strong similarity of shapes within the design. Many new stitch formations were introduced, and in any particular lace the mixture of stitches could be widely varied, giving a lively innovative air to the entire range.

When, in the mid-19th century, these antique laces were collected, studied, and to some extent revived, it became convenient to separate them into three distinct forms – Argentan, Argentella and Alençon – recognizable by the nature of their openwork grounds.

In Argentan lace, the hexagonal meshes characteristic of point de France and point de Sedan became smaller – 2mm (¹⁄₁₂in) across – and lost their picots. They were more uniform in size and more regular in shape. Each side was still covered by about 20 buttonhole stitches, and the result was called *brides bouclées* (literally, buttonholed bars).

Occasionally, small areas of decorative ground appeared filled with hexagons, each supporting internally a minute shape, like grubs nestling in a honeycomb. In some examples, these hexagonal *modes* spread throughout the entire openwork, creating a form of lace known as Argentella, characterized by a ground of *réseau rosacé* (rosette network).

Another stitch which first appeared as a rempli and finally extended to form the entire openwork ground, was *réseau ordinaire* (ordinary network), now regarded as a distinctive feature of Alençon lace. Rows of tbs were spaced apart and alternated with lightly whipped returns, preserving the hexagonal form of the meshes.

A fourth ground, known as *brides tortillées* (twisted bars), was a labour-saving form of brides bouclées, the buttonholing being replaced by a thread twisted around the mesh sides. Historically, this ground was first associated with Argentan.

All these forms were established between 1720 and 1740, but Argentan remained the Court favourite until the 1770s. Other new developments in the rempli included the absence of lining loops, and modes consisting of square buttonholed grids bordered with picots.

The detail is taken from a court lappet, c1760. No commercial Argentan lace was made from the end of the 18th century until, at the end of the 19th, the firm of Lefébure, in Bayeux, produced some fine exhibition pieces. These ceased with World War I. Today, the nuns of the Abbaye Notre Dame have revived the tradition.

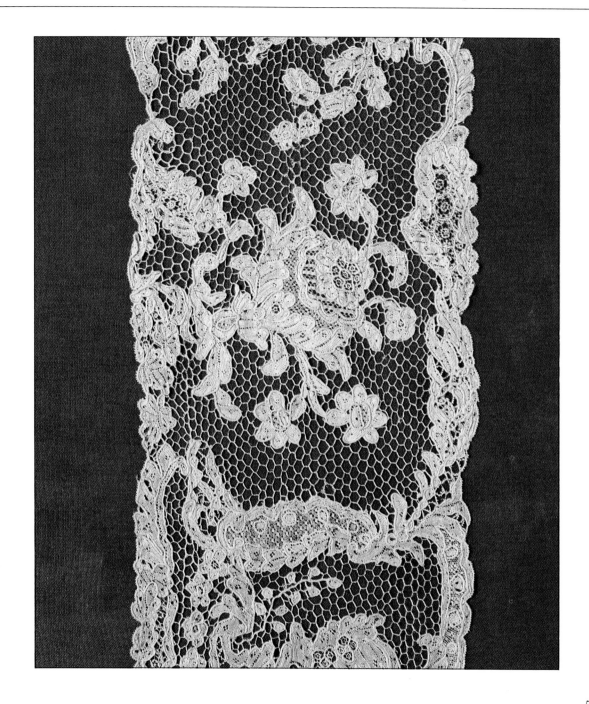

ARGENTAN 1 Portes and quadrilles
A Portes and quadrilles are found
in the solid design areas (dbs with
an sr), a quadrille being a group of
4 portes. The portes begin in a st
row, and a tbs may be used in the
middle and at the R-hand side to
enlarge the opening.

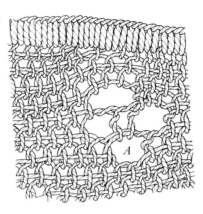

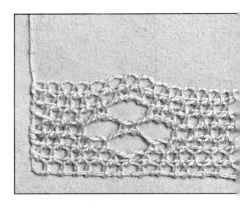

Rows 1–3 Dbs; sr; dbs.
Row 4 Pass the return thread
through the loops of the 3 middle
sts.
Row 5 Dbs, missing the 3 middle
sts and leaving a tallish loop (A)
above them.

Row 6 Secure the return thread by
passing it through the loop between
the 2 sts on either side of the
middle 3.

Row 7 Dbs, missing the 2 sts
marked out in row 6. Work 2 sts
(dbs or tbs) into loop A. Miss 2 sts.
Dbs to the end.
Continue as shown in the drawing.

B Openings may appear in larger
groupings, such as the 9-hole
diamond shown on the right, which
is formed in a similar manner to
the quadrille of Argentan 1A.

The dashes represent tall loops left
over missed sts.
Pins or couching sts, which will be
removed later, can be used to hold
the loop in place if necessary.
If 2 sts are substituted for 3 over
each tall loop, a more airy effect is
produced.
Sometimes the entire area of dbs is
studded with regularly arranged
quadrilles, making a light and
attractive decoration.

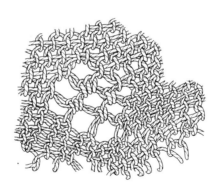

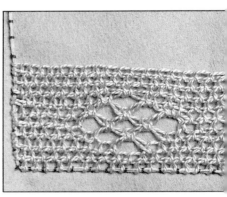

15	1	1	1	1	1	1	1	1	1	1	1	1	1	1	1	1	1		
13		1	1	1	1	1	1	1	–	–	1	1	1	1	1	1	1		
11		1	1	1	1	1	–	–	1	1	1	–	–	1	1	1	1		
9		1	1	–	–	1	1	1	–	–	1	1	1	–	–	1	1		
7	1	1	1	1	1	–	–	1	1	1	–	–	1	1	1	1			
5		1	1	1	1	1	1	1	–	–	1	1	1	1	1	1	1		
3	1	1	1	1	1	1	1	1	1	1	1	1	1	1	1	1			
1		1	1	1	1	1	1	1	1	1	1	1	1	1	1	1	1		

ARGENTAN 2 Veins and partitions

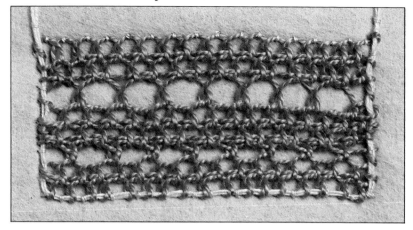

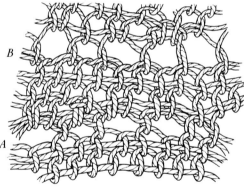

B Four rows make the vein:
Row 1 Whip the return thread through each alternate loop of the previous row. These loops will be missed in row 2.
Rows 2 and 3 As rows 5 and 6 of 2A.
Row 4 Finally, work 2 dbs into every loop of row 2.

Note: there are irregularities in the antique lace.

C The vein can be widened into a partition by adding additional twists to the dbs of Argentan 2B to make them taller.

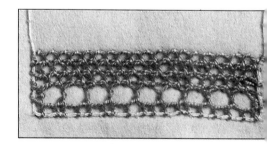

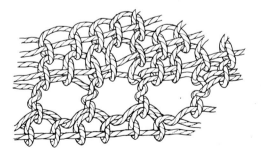

A In the solid design areas, narrow veins are used to separate the petals of a flower cluster or to divide a block of curling fronds into more delicate tendrils. Technically, these narrow veins are lines of portes separated by spaced dbs.
Rows 1–3 Dbs; sr; dbs.
Row 4 Take the sr fairly loosely back to the L side.
Row 5 Work dbs into every alternate st of row 3, leaving fairly wide loops between.
Row 6 Sr.

Row 7 Work 2 dbs into every loop of row 5, taking in also the threads of rows 4 and 6.
Continue in dbs with an sr to the next vein.

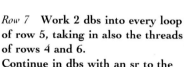

ARGENTAN 3

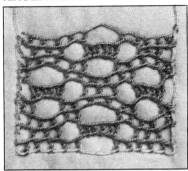

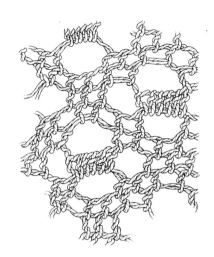

Work in contracted tbs with a
whipped return, but use extended
tbs where necessary to maintain the
shape of the pattern.

The clusters consist of 6 or 7 sts
packed tightly together.

The general sequence is shown in
the st diagram, and the curvature of
the rows in the drawing from the
antique lace, 12 rows forming a
complete pattern.

ARGENTAN 4

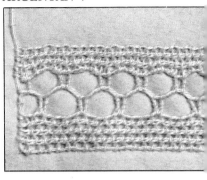

This is another way of lightening
solid areas of design.

Work 4 rows of dbs separated by 3
rows of sr. Make row 8 a whipped
return.

Row 9 Work a pair of extended tbs
with an extra twist into every 4th st
(5th loop) of row 7. Leave arched
loops between the pairs.

Row 10 Whipped return.

Row 11 Work a pair of tbs at the
mid-point of each arched loop.

Row 12 Either a straight or a
whipped return can be used.

Row 13 Work 4 dbs into each
arched loop of row 11, and 1 into
each short loop.

Work 4 rows of dbs, and repeat
rows 9 to 13.

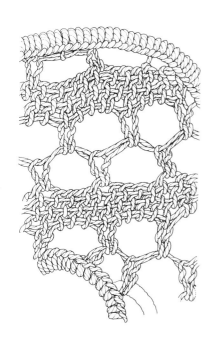

ARGENTAN 5

Here, areas of dbs are striped with open spaces, which are crossed by zigzag bars, buttonholed over and fringed with Venetian picots. A popular variation of this stitch form, used as a filling, consists of an irregular cross-hatching with the threads buttonholed over and lined with picots.

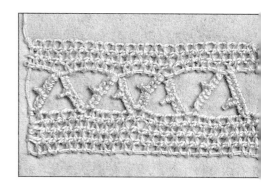

Work 4 rows of dbs separated by srs. Whip over the loops of the final row to make them firm.

Leave a gap slightly wider than 4 rows, then lay a tt across from X to Y. Work a further 4 rows of dbs, separated by srs.

Using this basis, link the two areas together with a double supporting thread, passed between them in a zigzag manner. Work back again, buttonholing L–R and R–L along alternate bars, adding a number of Venetian picots as you go.

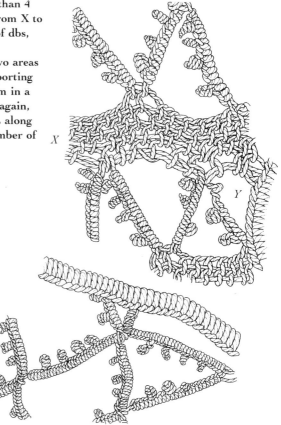

ARGENTAN 6 Flower centres

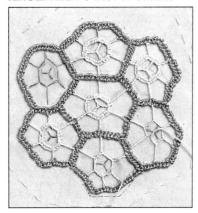

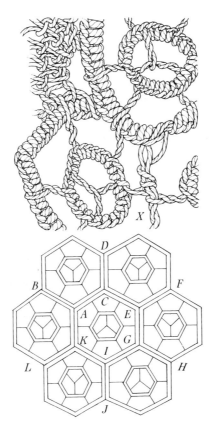

A   To practise, copy the shape and fix the pattern to the support with self-adhesive acetate film.
In the lace, the surrounding petals would have already been worked and the shape would be outlined by their tts.

The outside   Starting at A, couch a strand of sewing thread along the outline to B. Buttonhole back to A. Couch the strand to C, then D. Buttonhole from D to C. Couch to E, then F; buttonhole back to E. Continue in this way until you have returned to A, then buttonhole all around the inner hexagon, from A via C, E, G, I and K to A again. Couch a tt around the border of the outer hexagon and buttonhole over it.

The inside   Using a thinner thread, work six large tbs, one from the mid-point of each side, making their inner loops long enough to form the central shape. Hold them in position with couching stitches.

Take the thread of the final loop down into the middle and across to the far side as a tbs, then back to the third side, as shown, to make a 3-pronged centre.
Buttonhole around the central shape, with the needle pointing outwards. Finally, twist the thread around the initial strand, X, back to the outer hexagon.

B   Single hexagons may also be used as flower centres, the average size of each in the antique lace being 6.5mm (¼in).
Alternatively, a number may be grouped together to form an extensive filling.

Drawing the pattern   On graph paper, mark out dots, 2cm (¾in) apart, in a horizontal row.
Vertically up from these, mark dots at 2cm (¾in) and 1cm (⅜in) intervals and join them together. Midway between these vertical lines, draw a series of lines 1cm (⅜in) long to form the vertical sides of the hexagons.
The series of hexagons can be photocopied or traced and used as a pattern.

To make the flower centre   Outline the hexagon with a double tt. It will be left naked, not hidden beneath a cordonnet.

ARGENTAN 7 Ground of brides bouclées

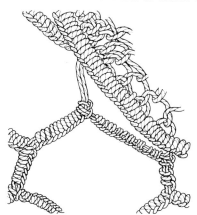

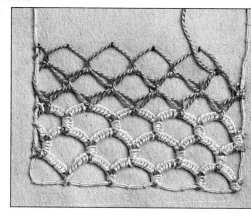

Work a lining layer of loops, 3 to each side and 1 across each corner (total 24 sts). Whip over the loops. Work groups of 3 extended tbs into each of the 3 loops along each side (18 groups). Whip over the loops. Work a suspending tbs from the middle of each side, couching their inner loops to form a central hexagon (total 6 sts).

Whip around this central hexagon, then buttonhole over the padding with the needle pointing outwards. As you go, work 2 Venetian picots in each segment (total 12).

Inside the central hexagon, work 6 short tbs.

Finally, return to the supporting thread that was left single, and twist around it, back to the outside.

Though the meshes are on a much smaller scale, the ground can be worked in a similar manner to point de France 11, but omitting the picots. An alternative method – filling the space with large dbs then buttonholing over the mesh sides – produces a curvature similar to that found in Youghal lace, rather than the sharp angles characteristic of Argentan.

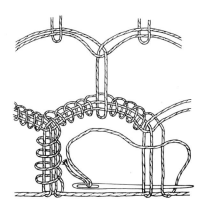

ARGENTAN 8 Cordonnet or brode

Lay several padding strands over the tt which outlines the motifs. Using a thickish thread, buttonhole closely along this padding. Traditionally, this work was carried out by attaching one end of the padding strands to the lace by 2 firm sts, and the other end to the lacemaker's belt so that it was held taut.

The *brodeuse* made several close buttonhole sts over the padding, before passing the needle beneath the tt, and working a further 2 buttonhole sts to secure it. In this way, while the entire padding was covered with buttonhole sts, it was attached to the tt only at intervals. For a right-handed person it is easier to work in a R–L direction, the right hand making the sts, the left holding the strands.

59

Argentan necklet

The antique motifs on which the design is based had to be modified, both because of the problems of fitting complex stitches into relatively small enclosures, and because modern threads were used. Note the radiating stitch rows on the cap of the poppy capsule, and their graceful curvature in the leaf segments. Each outline is covered with slightly padded close buttonhole stitching.

Threads
The threads used were as follows: solid design areas, linen; filling stitches, 100/3 silk.

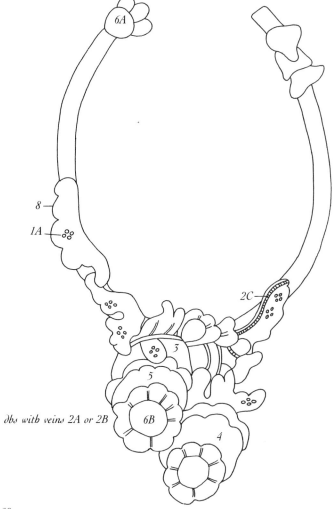

8

1A

2C

3

∂bs with veins 2A or 2B

6A

8

6B

5

4

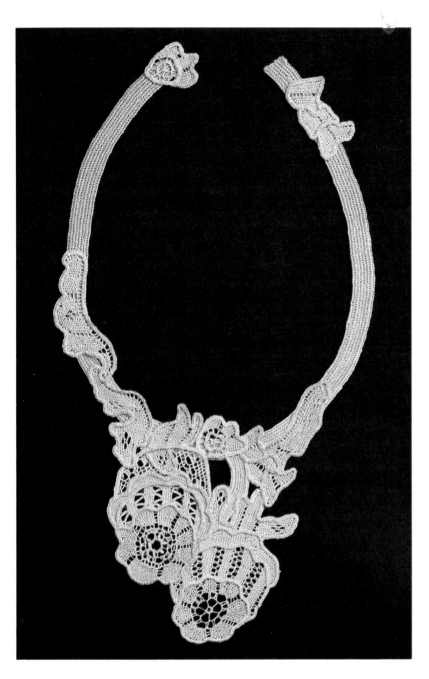

Worked by Sheila Ashby, the necklet design of fruits resembling poppy heads is based on motifs in the antique lace, but modified to show a variety of stitches.

ARGENTELLA

Argentella, the lace with the rosette ground, had probably developed by 1730, though perhaps not under that name. It may have been associated with the village of Argentelles, not far from Argentan. The *modes* of hexagonal rosettes now formed the main openwork ground of the lace. Réseau ordinaire, which had appeared as a rempli in point de Sedan and Argentan, was now extended to small areas of decorative ground enclosing clusters of flowers.

In the designs, buds, petals, leaves, fungi, even ferns, were represented in a naive semi-naturalistic manner that was saved from crudity only by the extreme fineness of the thread. The solid design areas of dbs with a straight return were once again stabbed through with portes arranged as quadrilles. Petals and leaflets were segmented by wide and narrow veining.

For the first time dbs appeared in fillings as well as in the solid areas of design, and tbs was worked in its extended rather than its contracted form.

Clusters reappeared, spaced apart by wide arched loops so that they conveyed the appearance of tiny bricks held apart by a filigree of wrought ironwork. In these areas, the return thread was whipped around the loops only as much as was necessary to keep the cavities clear.

As with other French laces, the cordonnet was closely covered with buttonhole stitches, worked in thicker thread. It was not in fact unusual for several different thread thicknesses to appear in a single lace, and there were in addition spontaneous variations in diameter of the handspun linen thread.

The outer border of the lace was fringed with tiny Venetian picots.

An unusual feature of this lace was the occasional appearance of lining loops around the solid design areas, especially where they adjoined each other.

Section of a court lappet, c1750

ARGENTELLA 1

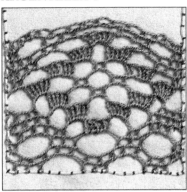

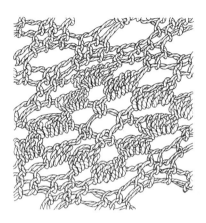

ARGENTELLA 2

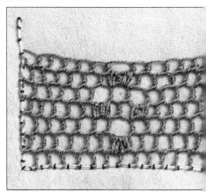

A new departure in some of the decorative areas of Argentella is the replacement of tbs by dbs, leaving tbs to form compacted clusters that stand like keystones over wide arched loops. In the antique lace, strong arching of the loops produced a sinuous curvature of the rows. In addition, the whole filling may have a diagonal slant. The entire diamond measures only 5mm

× 3mm (⅕in × ⅛in).
The stitch diagram shows the arrangement to be followed. The shaded blocks are clusters; the dashes represent holes, and the single vertical lines dbs.
The return thread is mainly straight, but whipped through the larger loops to keep the openings clear.

The basic stitch is an open arrangement of tbs with an additional twist. The return thread is whipped twice through each loop. The scattered *mouches* are worked on the return row. Take the thread down over a mesh of the previous row and fill it with needleweaving by passing the needle over-under the upper and lower sides several times.
The *mouches* may be arranged singly or, more commonly, in spaced-out diamond shapes.

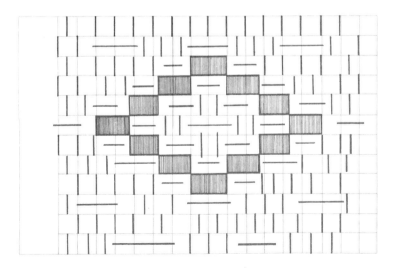

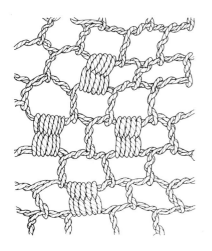

ARGENTELLA 3

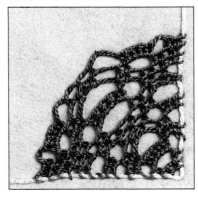

The dbs area is diapered with groups of 6 tbs compacted into clusters.

The rows are slanted diagonally to the space, but the clusters are vertically in line with each other. The even rows are the R–L whipped return rows, and 12 rows form the pattern.

Rows

11	–	3	–	6	–	3	–	6	–	3	–
9	2	2	2	–	2	2	2	–	2	2	2
7	2	–	2	2	2	–	2	2	2	–	2
5	–	6	–	3	–	6	–	3	–	6	–
3	2	–	2	2	2	–	2	2	2	–	2
1	2	2	2	–	2	2	2	–	2	2	2

In a variation of this stitch, shown below, the clusters are made of 5 tbs.

Rows

9	5	–	3	–	5	–	3	–	5	–	3	–
7	–	2	2	2	–	2	2	2	–	2	2	–
5	–	3	–	3	–	3	–	3	–	3	–	3
3	3	–	5	–	3	–	5	–	3	–	5	–
1	2	2	–	2	2	2	–	2	2	2	–	2

ARGENTELLA 4

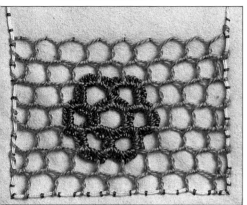

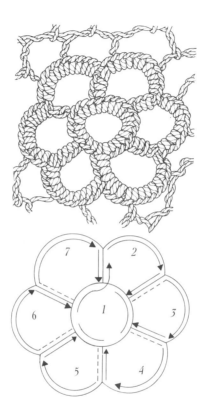

Fill the area with extended tbs with whipped returns, spaced apart to form meshes (*réseau ordinaire*). Select a mesh to serve as the centre. Buttonhole around it, using a slightly thicker thread, and then buttonhole the 6 surrounding meshes, with the needle pointing outwards as shown in the drawing. Follow the order 1 to 7.

To avoid overlapping the sts at the inner end of each 'petal', take the needle back up again to the point of junction with the next.

ARGENTELLA 5

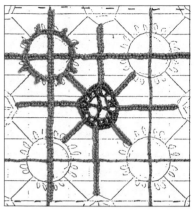

This filling is built up of alternating rows of circles and octagons. Enlarge the diagram to make the pattern.

Couch double tracing, or sewing, threads along lines AA, BB, to make a grid of squares.

Buttonhole over the grid, binding the tts together at each crossing point.

Couch a single tt around each intersection to form the *circles*. Buttonhole around the circumference, with the needle pointing outwards. Work 2 or 4 Venetian picots in each quadrant as you go (total 8 or 16).

The *octagon* hangs like a spider suspended from 8 rays linking it to circles and octagons as shown. Outline the octagon with a couched tt and line it with a row of 18 tbs. Whip over their inner loops.

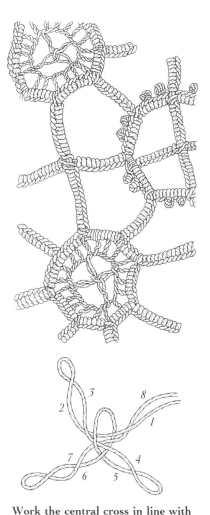

Work the central cross in line with AA and BB, following the numbers shown in the diagram.

Link the octagon to the circles by taking the sewing thread outwards to loop over the circumference, then buttonholing back to the octagon and around its perimeter to the next 'arm'. Repeat until all 4 arms are covered.

ARGENTELLA 6 The ground stitch

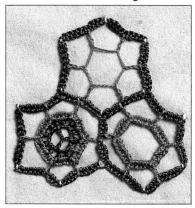

In the antique lace, the hexagons of the ground, which was known as *réseau rosacé* or rosette ground, are like the cells of a honeycomb, but slightly irregular since they were judged by eye alone. Draw a group of 3 or more hexagons and use this as the pattern.

Using the couching thread, work a hoop at each corner of every hexagon. Take a sewing thread through the hoops, and buttonhole along the sides, as described in point de France 11.

Work a lining layer of 6 large tbs inside each hexagon. Whip twice around their inner loops to strengthen them and provide a padding. Line this central hexagon with 12 tbs, 2 from each side. Whip over their inner loops.

Work the central tripod as shown, following the sequence 1–7.

Buttonhole over the padding of the central hexagon with the needle pointing outwards.

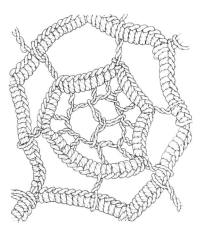

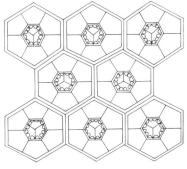

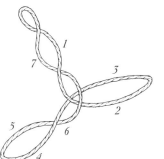

ARGENTELLA 7

All the hexagons of this filling are alike. For the sample, couch a double sewing thread to outline a single hexagon. Work a lining layer of extended tbs, 6 or 7 per side, spaced apart and hung over the outline. Whip through their inner loops to firm them.

Go around a 3rd time, working a dbs over each loop. At each corner take the thread across the angle in a short arc, pass it through a loop on the far side, then buttonhole back. Continue buttonholing to the next corner, and repeat, all the way round. Whip through each dbs loop. Draw the central circle on the pattern. Attach a sewing thread to one of the corner arcs and take it down to the circle. Couch it to the drawn outline; carry it out to the arc again, and then buttonhole back to the circle. Couch the thread around the circle to a point halfway towards the next arc, then take the thread across to the hexagon lining, and buttonhole back. Continue in this way until you are back to the beginning (12 buttonholed rays in all).

Take the thread around the circumference of the circle once or twice to pad it a little, then buttonhole over it with the needle pointing outwards, at the same time working a small Venetian picot in each of the 12 segments. Line the circle with about 12 extended tbs with an extra twist. Whip through their loops. Remove the couching stitches that support the circle, and make a tripod in the centre as in Argentella 6.

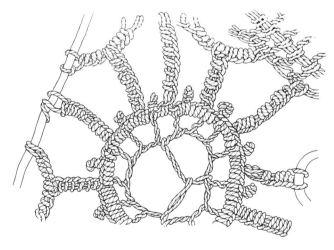

ARGENTELLA 8

The pattern consists of large hexagons with a circle or ring at every corner, and a smaller hexagon in the centre. The larger and smaller hexagons, the rings, and all the linking bars are made of two or more tts buttonholed over.

Smaller hexagons   Every side bears a ring picot. The loops of the centre 6 tbs are whipped around to make a circle and then lightly buttonholed over, with the needle facing inwards. This circle has 2 or 3 Venetian picots on each of its 6 segments.

To work the sample   Enlarge the diagram and use one or more large hexagons as the pattern. Couch tracing or sewing threads along the outline of the large hexagon and buttonhole over them.
The rings at the corners are most easily worked on a ring stick, making the Venetian picots at the same time. Wind the sewing thread fairly loosely around the stick about 6 times, then take the needle beneath this padding and work buttonhole sts around it.
Take the thread back through the first st. Ease the ring off the stick, and flatten it by pulling its rim gently downwards. Attach the ring at the hexagon corners with small stab stitches.
If a ring stick is not available, you can use any cylindrical support of appropriate size, such as a knitting needle or even a nail. Alternatively, couch a tt for each circle, pad it, and buttonhole over it.

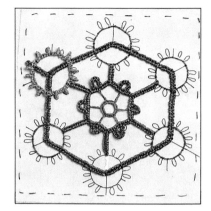

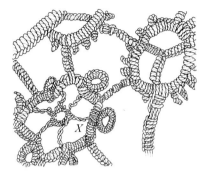

The smaller hexagon   Couch a tt along its outline. Attach a sewing thread to one of its angles; take it across to the nearest ring, and buttonhole back. Continue along the side of the hexagon to the next corner, working a ring picot on the way. Take the thread across to the nearest ring, and buttonhole back. Continue in this way until 6 rays have been worked and the outline of the smaller hexagon is covered in buttonholing with 6 ring picots. Fill in the centre by suspending 6 tbs from its inner side, beginning at X. Whip over their inner loops, and buttonhole over this padding with the needle inwards or outwards. Finally, twist back along the single thread to X, and finish off.

ARGENTELLA 9

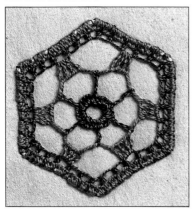

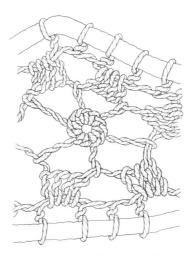

ARGENTELLA 10

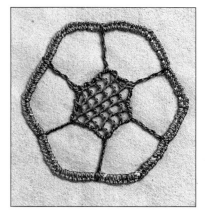

This formation occurs in isolation, as a flower centre. It is worked later than the other fillings, its stitches passing over the completed cordonnet.

Draw a hexagon and cover the outline with several tts. Buttonhole closely over them with the needle pointing towards the centre.

Line the cavity with wide-looped tbs slung over, or piercing through, the cordonnet, about 6 per side. Continue around a second time, whipping the thread over the loops to make them firm.

Work 6 clusters of 4 tbs over these loops, at equal intervals. Whip around again, passing the thread under and over every loop.

Hang 6 long loosely-twisted tbs from the loops between the 6 clusters. Hold their inner ends in position with couching stitches. Weave once or twice around their inner borders, then buttonhole over this central ring.

A   Plot a series of hexagons and buttonhole along their sides as described for Argentella 6.

All the hexagons are alike, so for the sample only one need be worked. From X, hang an extended tbs over the mid-point of each side, into the middle. Couch the inner loops and whip once around them, making a small central hexagon. Finish by twisting the thread back to X.

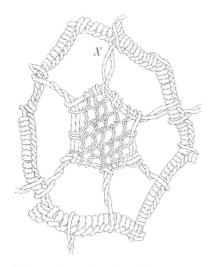

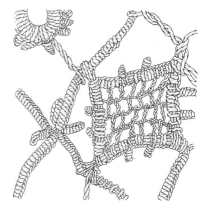

Using a finer thread, work 5 rows of extended tbs with whipped returns across this inner hexagon, passing the thread around the sides at the end of every row.

B   The framework is a straight-sided grid, placed diagonally. Couch down tt intersecting at right angles across the space to be filled (AA, BB). Buttonhole over this grid, working 4 large Venetian picots at each intersection.
The diamond-shaped frames enclose alternating rows of squares and circles.

Circles   Suspend 4 large tbs, one from the middle of each side of the frame. Whip a thread 2 or 3 times around their inner loops and then buttonhole over them with the needle pointing outwards, working 2 or 3 small Venetian picots in each quadrant.

Squares   Pass several strands of tt over the mid-points of the sides of the frame to form a square. Buttonhole around this square with the needle pointing outwards,

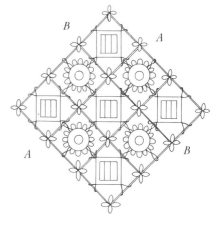

working 2 Venetian picots on each side.
Fill the square with 4 rows of extended tbs with whipped returns.

C   In a simpler form of the above, the diamond-shaped frames are empty and undecorated, except for bunches of 4 Venetian picots at every corner.

Cushion centre

The central motif has been left incomplete to show the course of the tracing threads that outline the different areas. The surrounding wedges will be worked with stitches, as numbered, and each hexagon of stitch 5 filled, as in the original. Every outline is emphasized with a buttonholed cordonnet, lightly padded. If the project is to be mounted on a cushion, choose the backing fabric carefully, so that it enhances the colour scheme.

Threads

The threads used were as follows: tts, mercer crochet single 20, or double 40; flowers and quatrefoils, Madeira rayon machine embroidery thread 40; fruits and toadstools, stitch 3, and the cordonnet of the finer areas, 100/3 silk; solid design areas of the leaves, and sts 2 and 5, mercer crochet 60.

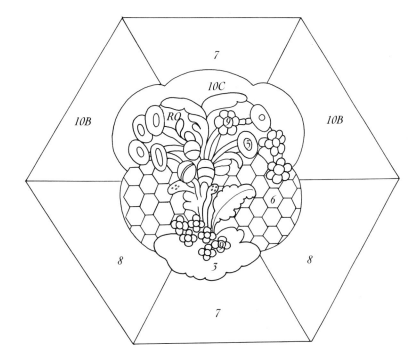

For this cushion centre, worked by the author, the central motif was taken direct from the 18th-century lappet, and set in a frame that echoes the distinctive hexagons of Argentella.

ALENÇON

Alençon lace has a ground of *réseau ordinaire* (sometimes called *tulle*), worked in very fine thread. It is also distinguished by its decoration of numerous little picots projecting like thorns from the slightly raised and closely buttonholed cordonnet. In the late 18th century, these picots were made by taking the thread over a black horsehair to ensure that they were equal in size. The hair was withdrawn as each picot was completed.

Alençon was the lightest of the French needlelaces, replacing Argentan as Court favourite in the last quarter of the 18th century. In 1804 it was resurrected by Napoleon I, but demand dwindled following his defeat in 1815. Several decades later the Empress Eugénie, wife of Napoleon III, reintroduced it to fashion – with changes. The heavier *brides tortillées* were now used to give weight and substance to a lace forced to compete with the lavish ostentation of the period. Sharp borders of picots were supported over white horsehair, and this was left in, probably couched to the pattern during manufacture. Loop picots were used more extensively, replacing the time-consuming Venetian ones.

Also during the 1850s, manufacturers finally overcame their prejudice against cotton thread, which had already been in use for bobbin and machine laces for over 20 years.

By 1880, some 36 different filling stitches were in common use. Many took the form of tiny circles, represented simply by 'O'. Picots were called 'noses' (*nez*). Thus *O à nez* would be 'a circle with picots'; *O à nez en queue*, 'circle with picots in a line, or queue'; *O en chainettes*, 'circles in chains'; *couronnes d'O bouclé*, 'crowns of buttonholed circles'; *étoile à double nez*, 'a star with a double row of picots'.

Between 1900 and 1914, some superb pieces of Alençon lace were commissioned from the firm of Lefebure at Bayeux, such as a handkerchief with a deep lace border for the Empress of Russia, but this *belle époque* was cut off sharply by the outbreak of World War I. The lace continued to be made, albeit in a simplified manner, during the 1920s, and remained expensive.

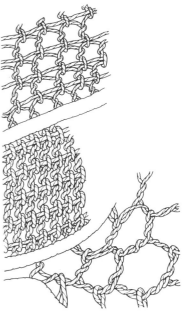

The shadow effect, introduced in 1855, was made with the same stitch – contracted tbs with a straight return – used throughout, but in the lighter areas the stitches were spaced apart and worked in thinner thread.

Section of a court lappet, c1770

ALENÇON 1

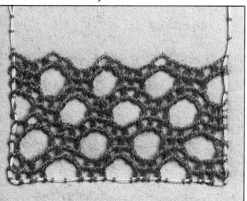

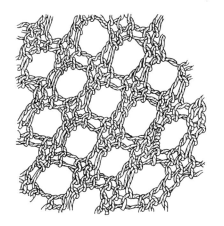

ALENÇON 2

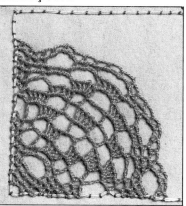

The entire filling is worked in dbs. The return thread (even rows) is whipped once through each loop. The stitch arrangement is slightly staggered in successive rows, and the large holes are in line diagonally but not vertically.

Row 1 Work 3 sts. °Overpass the next 3 sts with a balloon-like loop. Work 3 sts. Repeat from ° to the end. Use pins to support the larger loops and to keep them equal in size, or stretch a temporary thread across the space to hold them up.

Row 3 Dbs right across, working 2 sts above every group of 3, and 3 sts into the top of every balloon.

Row 5 Work a st, leave a balloon loop over the next 3 sts, work a st into each of the next 3 loops, and continue in this way to the end.

In the sample, the filling has been worked horizontally to clarify the sequence. In the antique lace the rows are worked diagonally.

In a background of dbs, 13 clusters of extended tbs are grouped in a diamond shape.

Starting at X on the drawing, work diagonally across the space to be filled.

Rows

```
11   1 1 1 1 1 1 1 1 1 1 1 1 1 1 1 1 1
 9   - 1 1 1 - - 1 1 1 - - 1 1 1 - - 1 1
 7   1 1 1 1 1 1 1 1 1 1 1 1 1 1 1 1 1 1
 5   1 - - 1 1 1 - - 1 1 1 - - 1 1 1 - -
 3   1 1 1 1 1 1 1 1 1 1 1 1 1 1 1 1 1 1
 1   1 1 1 - - 1 1 1 - - 1 1 1 - - 1 1 1
```

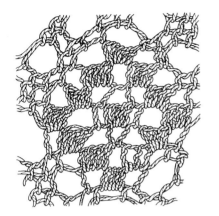

ALENÇON 3

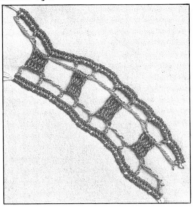

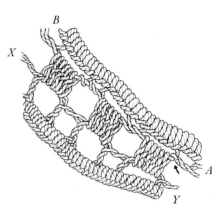

The stitch is intended to link together two distinct areas by needleweaving. In the lace, the tts on either side of the gap would be used as bases for the attachment of the stitches.

For the sample, couch 2 tts approximately parallel to each other.
Work a row of tbs, spaced apart, over each tt, so that their wide loops are lined up opposite each other.
Whip the thread back through the loops of XY, but not through AB. Buttonhole over the tt as shown in the drawing.
Attach the sewing thread at A, and needleweave across and back between alternate loops, following the direction indicated in the sketch.

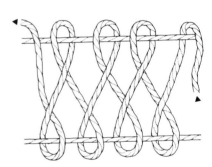

ALENÇON 4

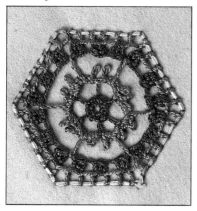

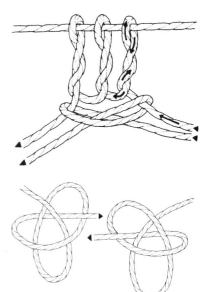

This stitch is similar to Argentan 6B, but with three differences. The first is found in the central ring, which in Argentan is simply the inner loops of 6 tbs. In Alençon, the loops are run through with two or three circles of thread, then buttonholed over with the needle pointing towards the centre. Secondly, Alençon does not use buttonholed Venetian picots but a simpler looped form, in which a loop is made outwards from the buttonholed rim and the base is gripped together with a tight overhand knot.

Finally, the 3-st clusters do not have the whipped return passing through every loop. Instead, the thread from the last loop turns back on itself, passing through the loop between the clusters, then on again, in effect binding the first and last sts of each cluster together.

To work the sample, first lay down one or more hexagons by couching triple tts along their outline. These are left bare of any close covering. Hang a lining layer of contracted tbs over them, 6 per side. These will alternate with similar lining sts in the adjoining hexagons. Whip the thread through the loops of the lining layer all the way around to tighten them.

Work 18 groups of 3 tbs (3 groups per side) through alternate lining loops, binding the first and last sts together.

Sling a long tbs over the loop at each corner of the hexagon and catch their inner borders with couching thread so that they outline an *inner hexagon*. Overcast its outline with padding strands, then buttonhole over them with the needle pointed outwards, and work 2 loop picots on each side.

The couching sts of the inner hexagon can now be removed. Within its frame, suspend a long tbs from the mid-point of each side. Where their loops almost meet in the centre, whip around them to make a ring. Buttonhole over the ring with the needle pointing inwards.

Loop picot – a knot can be tied at the base of the loop, in either direction.

ALENÇON 5

This formation consists of rosettes of hexagons, 6 clustered around a central 7th. Winding between the rosettes is a pathway of single hexagons, empty of contents except for 6 inwardly-directed loop picots, like plain flagstones encircling and separating the more decorative areas.

The central hexagon of each rosette is also empty except for its loop picots, but the 6 surrounding ones have buttonholed rings in their middles, hung in the usual manner from 6 long tbs.

Begin the sample by constructing a series of hexagons as for Argentan 6.

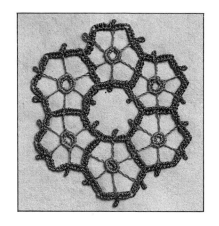
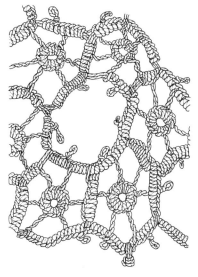

ALENÇON 6

Copy the pattern and fix it to the supporting cloth. Lay a square grid of tracing or sewing threads, and fix them as necessary with couching sts. Add a diagonal grid passing through alternate intersections. Buttonhole over all of them. Couch a diamond-shaped outline where 4 grid threads cross, and a circle where 8 grid threads cross. Buttonhole around the *diamond* with the needle pointing outwards, and work 3 loop picots on each side as you go, taking the thread over the 4 lines of the square grid.

Buttonhole around the *circle* with the needle pointing outwards, taking the thread over the 8 radii.

Once the diamonds and circles are complete, their couching sts can be removed.

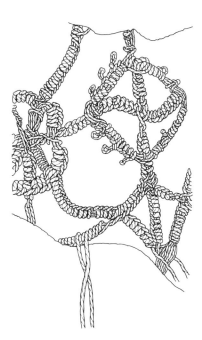

ALENÇON 7 O en chainettes

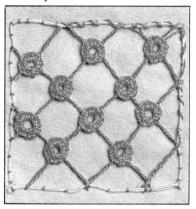

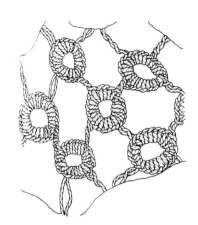

Make a grid of paired threads crossing diagonally to fill the area with diamond shapes. At each crossing insert a needle and ease the threads apart.

Oversew them with couching thread to hold them in place. Buttonhole around the central hole to make a circle.

Pass from one circle to the next by whipping over the pair of threads between them.

ALENÇON 8 O à nez en chainettes

Proceed as for Alençon 7, though the grid lines may be horizontal and vertical to the area instead of diagonal.

As you buttonhole around each circle, work 2 Venetian picots (*nez*) in each quadrant.

Advance to the next circle by whipping or buttonholing over the paired threads.

A supporting horsehair is enclosed by loop picots knotted tightly at the cordonnet.

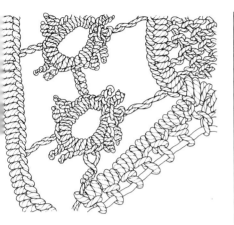

ALENÇON 9

A Alençon ground (*réseau ordinaire*)
This is the distinctive ground of
18th- and early 19th-century
Alençon laces. It was worked in a
finer thread than the other stitches,
forming a delicate foil for the
design.

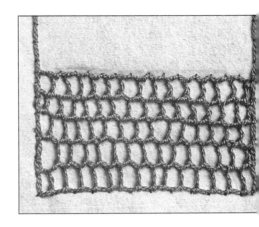

Rows of extended tbs are spaced
apart to make an openwork. The
whipped return is left slightly slack
so that the meshes can be eased
into a hexagonal shape as the
following row is worked.

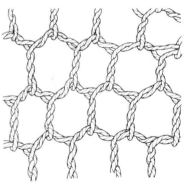

B In the 19th-century revival, the
heavier *brides tortillées* ground,
originally associated with Argentan,
was substituted for the *réseau
ordinaire* to create a more impressive
effect.
This ground is made by twisting a
sewing thread around all the sides
either of réseau ordinaire meshes
(tbs with a whipped return) or of
tall dbs with an sr.

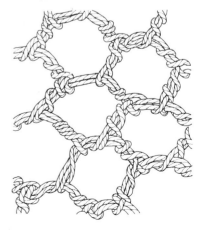

Floral motifs

The conventional carnation is worked almost entirely in dbs with a straight return, its reflexed and convoluted petals emphasized by a light cordonnet. Stitch 6, in the petal centres, is simplified. The composite flower head for the centre back has a circle added, for support. Part-rows have been used in the bracts, as in the petals, to preserve the general radiating lines of the stitch rows.

The two floral motifs, designed for a collar, were worked by the author and Joan Carter. They were selected from the antique lappet, and can be applied to net or other material, as indicated.

Threads

The threads used were: tts of the carnation, cordonnet special 40; tt of the composite, mercer crochet 10; other stitches, 100/3 silk.

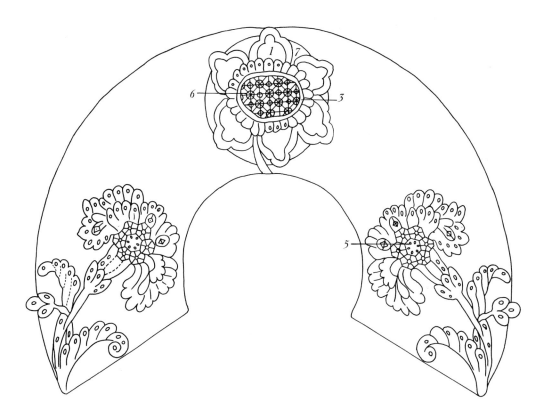

RESEAU VENISE

Réseau Venise is exceptionally fine and totally flat except for rare decorations of minutely padded rings. There is no cordonnet. The ground resembles that of Alençon, though the stitches may have an additional twist and are worked horizontally to the design – widthwise in a lappet, lengthwise in an edging. The whipped return thread is sometimes tightened, distorting the hexagonal meshes into a square shape, characteristic of later Burano laces.

The solid design areas are of dbs with a straight return, close form. There is a wide range of filling stitches, all built up of tbs. They spill over the lace in dramatically slanting lines, zigzags and diamond-shaped groupings, with tall loops leaping between the stitches to produce an exotic effect.

The oriental nuance of its designs links réseau Venise with point de Sedan, and the decorative rempli are lined with loops reminiscent of the earlier lace. The two laces appear in fact to be linked by intermediate forms, which have a meshwork ground similar to réseau Venise, but are slightly heavier, with a suggestion of padding strands laid over the tracing threads and held down by the loops of adjoining areas rather than by a separate covering of buttonhole stitches. Such laces are sometimes referred to as 'Brussels needlelace'. They are more closely textured than the 19th-century Brussels point de gaze, but that has a similar open padding, and both display areas where stitches are worked in every row, omitting the return threads.

Réseau Venise also resembles French laces. Its petals and pinnate fronds are narrow and curving, pierced at their tips with openwork quadrilles; the dbs run lengthwise of the shapes, with part-rows added or subtracted to follow the outline in a graceful manner; the outer border is fringed with minute Venetian picots. The exceptional fineness of the handspun linen thread places réseau Venise in the first half of the 18th century.

Section of a broad lappet of réseau Venise, c1740

RESEAU VENISE 1 Réseau ordinaire with rings

The tiny decorative rings have a diameter of only 1mm (¹⁄₂₄in) in the antique lace.

Lay a tt and line it all around with tbs loops. Whip around their inner borders. Fill the space within them with extended tbs with an additional twist. This makes the sides taller and enlarges the meshes.
To make the rings, use a thicker thread and whip around the sides of a single mesh to make a circular shape. Buttonhole over this padding.

RESEAU VENISE 2

This represents a new development, in so far as there are stitches in every row. It is found in the slightly heavier examples of réseau Venise, sometimes referred to as 'Brussels needlelace'. There are several varied groupings, but all consist of extended tbs worked in every row, L–R and R–L, the stitches of L–R rows having an additional twist. All loop closures are in a Z direction.
In the simpler formations there is a vestigial cordonnet, and no lining loops. In the more complex formations there are unwhipped lining loops, and no padding over the tt.
Some 4 variations of this stitch are shown opposite. In each case the odd rows are worked L–R, and the even rows R–L.

Note
In the following stitches (3 to 6 and their variations) the more usual arrangement of rows reappears, the stitch rows alternating with return thread rows.

Stitches in every row

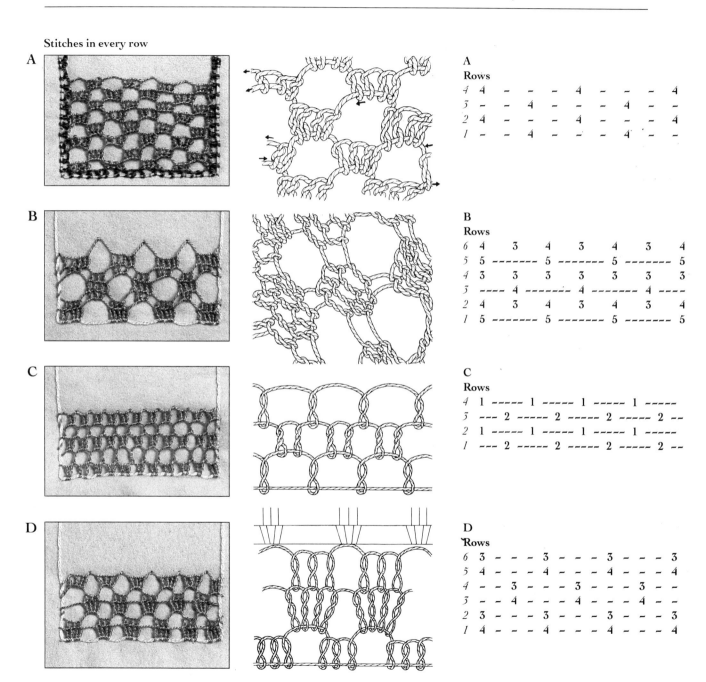

A

Rows

4	4	–	–	–	4	–	–	–	4
3	–	–	4	–	–	–	4	–	–
2	4	–	–	–	4	–	–	–	4
1	–	–	4	–	–	–	4	–	–

B

Rows

6	4	3	4	3	4	3	4
5	5	-------	5	-------	5	-------	5
4	3	3	3	3	3	3	3
3	----	4	-------	4	-------	4	----
2	4	3	4	3	4	3	4
1	5	-------	5	-------	5	-------	5

C

Rows

4	1	-----	1	-----	1	-----	1	-----
3	---	2	-----	2	-----	2	-----	2	--
2	1	-----	1	-----	1	-----	1	-----
1	---	2	-----	2	-----	2	-----	2	--

D

Rows

6	3	–	–	–	3	–	–	–	3	–	–	–	3
5	4	–	–	–	4	–	–	–	4	–	–	–	4
4	–	–	3	–	–	–	3	–	–	–	3	–	–
3	–	–	4	–	–	–	4	–	–	–	4	–	–
2	3	–	–	–	3	–	–	–	3	–	–	–	3
1	4	–	–	–	4	–	–	–	4	–	–	–	4

RESEAU VENISE 3 Diagonals with displacement: staggered lines

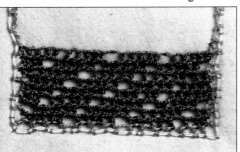

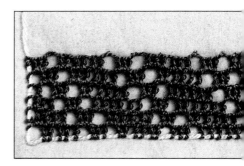

A The basic stitch is contracted tbs.

The return thread is straight except where it is passed around the loop between the 4th and 5th sts of each group. The rows are worked horizontally or diagonally across the enclosures.

Make a lining layer of loops.

Row 1 ° 5 tbs. Leave a space the width of 2 sts. Repeat from ° to end.

Row 3 ° Leave a space the width of 2 sts. Work 5 sts so that the final 2 are over the loop left in row 1. Repeat from ° to end.

Row 5 Work 2 tbs. ° Leave a space the width of 2 sts. 5 tbs. Repeat from ° to end.

Continue, so that the final 2 sts of every 5 are always above the loops left in the previous st row, giving the appearance of slanting lines separated by gaps. The angle of the slant can be increased by leaving gaps the width of 3 sts, and reduced by leaving gaps the width of 1 st. The slant can run in the opposite direction.

B The stitch is again contracted tbs. The return thread is whipped only through the loops that will be missed in the following row. The appearance is of alternating thick and thin diagonal stripes separated by slanting lines of holes.
The blocks can be staggered in either direction.

Row 1 ° 6 tbs. Miss a space the width of 2 sts. Work 3 tbs close together to occupy the space of 2 sts. Miss a space the width of 2 sts. Repeat from ° to end.
Repeat this st row throughout the area, but moving all sts two spaces to the left in each row. In this way, the cluster of 3 will always be over the gap left at the end of the block of 6 in the previous row, and the first 2 sts of each block of 6 will be over the gap to the right of the cluster of 3.

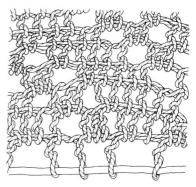

3A Rows

```
7        1 1 1 - 1 1 1 1 - 1 1 1 1 1 - 1 1
5      1 1 - 1 1 1 1 1 - 1 1 1 1 1 - 1 1 1 1
3        - 1 1 1 1 1 - 1 1 1 1 1 - 1 1 1 1 1
1      1 1 1 1 1 - 1 1 1 1 1 - 1 1 1 1 1 - 1
```

3B Rows

```
9    111 - 1 1 1 1 1 - 111 - 1 1 1 1 1 1 - 111
7    1 - 111 - 1 1 1 1 1 1 - 111 - 1 1 1 1 1 1 -
5    1 1 - 111 - 1 1 1 1 1 1 - 111 - 1 1 1 1 1
3    1 1 1 1 - 111 - 1 1 1 1 1 1 - 111 - 1 1 1 1
1     1 1 1 1 1 - 111 - 1 1 1 1 1 - 111 - 1 1 1
```

RESEAU VENISE 4

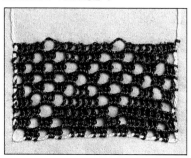

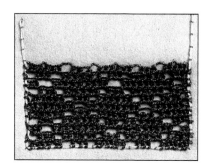

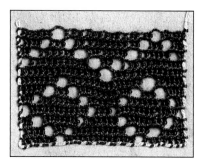

A   Double diamonds
The basic stitch is extended tbs.
The sr is whipped only through the loops that will be missed in the following row. The effect is of solid and pierced diamonds, alternating in horizontal bands.

B   Solid diamonds
This formation is worked lengthwise of the enclosure.
The stitches are arranged in solid diamond-shaped blocks, alternating vertically, and separated from each other by lines of holes.
The return thread (even rows) is straight, except where it whips over the gaps left between the groupings.

**C   As in 4B, solid diamond-shaped blocks alternate vertically with each other. Each is surrounded by an outline of holes, and in addition they are separated from each other by solid zigzag blocks that run between them in a horizontal direction. The return threads pass only through the loops that will be missed in the following row.

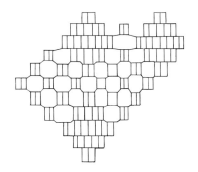

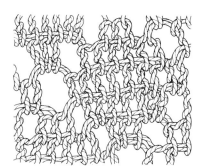

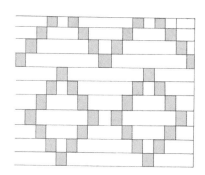

RESEAU VENISE 5 Chevrons

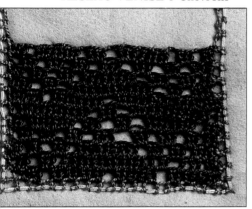

Solid and open zigzag stripes alternate with each other.

The sts are extended tbs with an additional twist.

The return thread is mainly straight, but is whipped through the loops of each of the 3 sts that will be passed over in the following row; 12 rows form the pattern.

RESEAU VENISE 6 Tilted squares

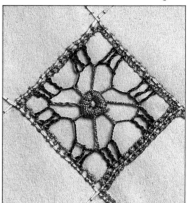

Line the entire enclosure with whipped loops.

Divide it into equal-sided diamonds and couch several strands of thin tt along their sides.

Hook a row of contracted tbs along the sides of the diamonds so that the sts of adjoining frames alternate with each other. (A similar technique is found in Alençon 4.) Do not whip over the loops.

Work 2 clusters of 3 tbs per side (total 8). Do not whip over their loops.

Starting at a corner loop (X), take the thread towards the centre and fix it with a couching st. Work round the 8 clusters, hanging a single tbs over each loop between them. Couch the inner end of each st thus made, leaving a small central hollow.

Rows

Row	Numbers
25	
23	3
21	3 3
19	3 3 3
17	3 8 3
15	12 3
13	8 8
11	12 12
9	8 8
7	3 3
5	
3	12 12
1	

☐ = space   *stitches arranged as numbered*

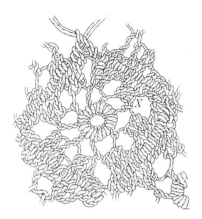

Weave the sewing thread in and out of these radii to make a padded ring. Buttonhole over it with the needle pointing inwards. Finally, twist the thread back along the single strand to X, and finish off.

Similar contents are sometimes found in hexagonal frames.

RESEAU VENISE 7 Triangles in hexagons

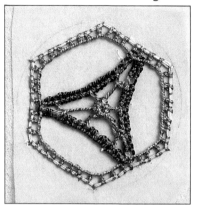

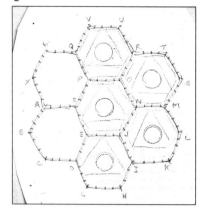

This stitch comes from the 18th-century 'Brussels needlepoint'. In the antique lace each hexagon measures 5mm (¼in) across.

Divide the area into hexagons as shown in Argentan 6.
Outline each hexagon with couched double tts, separating them into singles as required.
Beginning at the mid-point of one side, line the tts with contracted tbs. Continue around again, whipping over the loops.
On returning to the starting point, take a double thread to the mid-point of the opposite side, across to the 3rd side and back again, to form the triangle. Suspend long tbs from the corners and mid-points of each side, and fix their inner ends with couching sts. Run the needle in and out of these inner ends to make a light padding, then buttonhole over it, with the needle pointing inwards.
Cover the triangle sides with

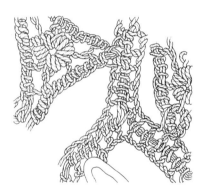

buttonhole sts, pointing the needle outwards.

RESEAU VENISE 8 The ground
This is similar to réseau ordinaire, but the extended tbs sometimes have an extra twist, making a lighter openwork. Also, the return thread whips 3 or 4 times through each loop and is often pulled tightly so that the meshes are distorted into small squares instead of being clearly 6-sided.

Necklace with pendant

Each plaque of the necklace is filled with a typical reseau Venise stitch, as numbered. Even so, some modifications were necessary, such as the use of contracted tbs instead of the extended form in stitch 5, and the simplification of some of the centres. Although the tt is fairly thick, there is no cordonnet.

Threads

The threads used were as follows: tt, Madeira metallic effect yarn, not doubled; lining loops, 3-strand fil argent clair; dbs, Madeira rayon 40; rings in the pendant, 1 strand of fil argent clair.

This necklace of plaques, complete with pendant, was worked by the author. Because of the extreme fineness of the original thread, it was almost impossible to lift a motif from the lappet illustrated and fit traditional stitches into it without enormous enlargement. A design was therefore taken direct from an 18th-century Argentan lace of mixed form, which combined decorative grounds of Argentella and Alençon with its own.

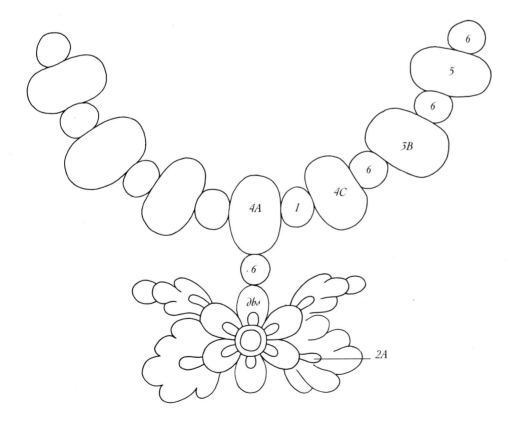

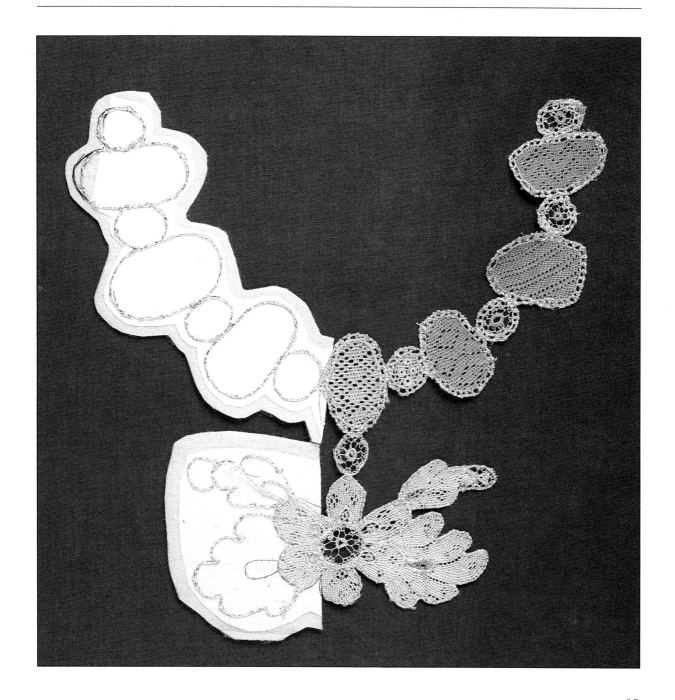

POINT DE GAZE (gauze lace)

The manufacture of point de gaze is traditionally associated with Brussels. The lace was first recorded in 1851, but in the late 18th century needlelace motifs of similar technique were worked in fine linen thread and applied to a hand-made net. However, before the middle of the 19th century, Flemish manufacturers of needlelace appear to have been subsidiaries of French firms, or subject to Italian direction.

Point de gaze introduced a number of new or ingeniously modified ideas, to make a frivolously pretty lace of naturalistic flowers caught in a gauzy web of tbs, worked in every row. The solid design areas were of dbs with a straight return, but worked in an open form, the stitches spaced apart to produce a lighter effect. Like Alençon, point de gaze used variations in stitch spacing and thread thickness to achieve perspective.

In the 1860s or 70s, separately attached petals were added to the flowers, enhancing their naturalness. Point de gaze also borrowed *modes* from Alençon lace, and elaborated on their circles, stars and rays, stringing them across the lace like chains of variegated beads. Small padded rings of graduated size radiated from the hearts of flowers and clustered within the petals, simulating a spiralling core of stamens. The outer borders of petals and modes were often scalloped with sprightly hoops of knotted buttonhole stitches, while loop picots sprang like haloes from woven knobs and padded rings.

The cordonnet, which in point de gaze is softer and less prominent than in Alençon, was left naked except for a light covering of spaced buttonhole stitches, or more simply its padding strands were trussed together by the loops of the outermost stitches of the enclosures which they encircled.

Top quality pieces of point de gaze were made of 440-count cotton thread, machine-spun in England. The manufacturers also catered for the lower end of the market with laces of simpler design and slacker texture, lacking both raised petals and buttonholed rings, and using thicker cotton (250 to 300 count) to minimize the cost. Today, Zele needlelace carries on many point de gaze traditions.

The distinctive features of point de gaze are shown here – the light airy ground with twisted stitches in every row (A), the open form of dbs (B), and the incompletely covered cordonnet strands (C).

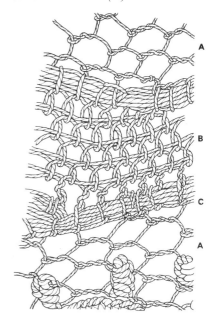

A detail of point de gaze, this shows the distinctive ground, design areas and cordonnet strands. Venetian picots are seen jutting out from a tightly buttonhole-stitched crown or couronne.

POINT DE GAZE 1

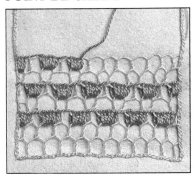

Fill the area with meshes of point de gaze ground. Then, in alternate rows, take a thicker thread and work clusters of 5 dbs along the top of every alternate mesh.

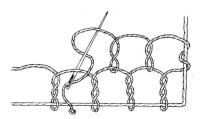

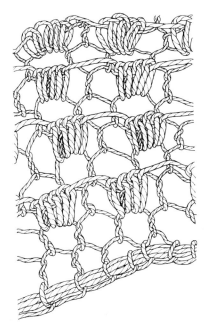

POINT DE GAZE 2

There are several versions of this stitch formation, but the basic structure is always a floret, its 8 petals frilled around with knotted buttonhole stitches.

In 2A, the floret is encased in a circle of padding strands, buttonholed over and linked by sinuous tracing threads to neighbouring circles of different content. In 2B, the florets are free of their encirclement, but massed together in ranks of regimental precision, interspersed with tiny rings, the whole chained together by short double strands. You may work straight or slantwise of the enclosure.

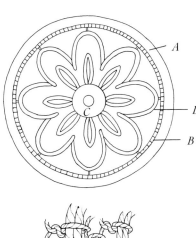

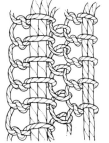

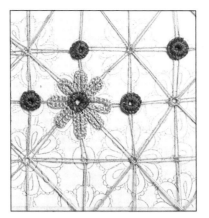

A   On your pattern paper, draw a circle (A) the required size. Divide it into 8 equal segments (45° for each). Draw a small circle for the central ring (C). Add petal shapes, placing the mid-line of each over one of the radii (D). Outline A with a firmly couched tt. Line it with a single row of tbs with a whipped return (B).

Lay padding strands over A. Cover them with wide buttonhole sts, pointing the needle outwards and passing it beneath the couched tt with each st. This is the *cordonnet*. Lightly couch padding strands along both inner and outer borders of the petals, leaving a cavity between. Link the inner strands to the tt of C.

Overstitch the outer and inner strands with knotted loops, set opposite each other so they are equal in number. Link the knotted loops together internally with a single row of dbs. Buttonhole closely over C, concealing the attachment to it of the petals.

B   Lay a thin grid of double horizontal and vertical threads crossed by diagonals at alternate intersections.

Put the needle in the centre of an intersection and gently separate the pairs of grid threads. Whip around them with a fine thread, binding them in position so that they cannot slip. This creates a clear central hole around which the buttonholed ring will be worked.

Where 4 threads cross, take the sewing thread round once or twice to make a thin padding, then buttonhole over with the needle pointing outwards.

Where 8 threads cross, construct a floret of 8 petals, as for stitch 2A. Use the surround of knotted buttonhole sts to bind the grid thread on each side to the padding.

Knotted buttonhole stitch   Work a dbs over the cordonnet. Pass the needle back beneath the point of closure and make a tight buttonhole stitch.

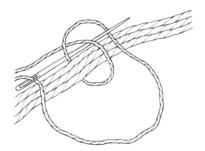

POINT DE GAZE 3

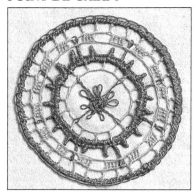

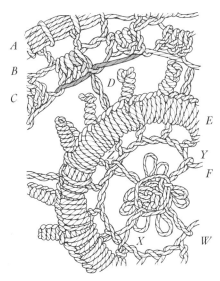

POINT DE GAZE 4

Draw 2 concentric circles, A and E. Couch a tt over each. Divide the outer circle into 8 equal parts to mark the position of the sts of stage 4.

Line the tt of A with a single layer of tbs, spaced apart, 4 per octant (total 32). Overcast each loop once. In alternate loops of row 2, work 4 tbs close together, to give 16 clusters. Whip over the loops between the clusters.

Hang 8 large loosely-twisted sts (D) from B along the 8 radii drawn at the beginning. Pass the thread beneath C. Take it along tt E to the next position, then back to B. Two of the clusters of C will lie between these sts.

End by twisting around the single starting thread back to B.

Next, work 16 contracted tbs inside E, spacing them to alternate with the clusters C. Whip once over each loop to make a firm edge.

The central decoration   Select a point, X, on F, midway between two of the sts from D. Take the thread across to the far side, Y, hoop it over a loop of F, twine it back to the centre, and knot the threads together.

Next, centre to Z; Z to W; W to centre. Work a woven knob (see point de gaze 5). Work 2 large loop picots in each quadrant, knotting their bases tightly. Twist back along the single strand to X.

Lay padding strands over E and cover them with close buttonhole sts. Add 8 Venetian picots as indicated.

Finally, lay padding strands over A, and secure them to the tt with spaced dbs.

Draw a grid of paired lines diagonally across the space to be filled, spacing the pairs as shown in the diagram. Lay threads along these lines.

At each intersection, couch the threads in position, slightly apart, leaving a small space in the centre. Darn in and out of the grid at these crossings to make a light padding, then buttonhole over the padding to form a ring. Link the rings together by whipping over one of the grid threads between them. The couching sts can be removed as soon as the ring is complete.

Work 2 groups of 4 large dbs over each pair of threads forming the sides of the diamonds.

Cross the central cavity of the diamond with tbs. Weave around their middle to form a raised knob with 4 loop picots.

POINT DE GAZE 5

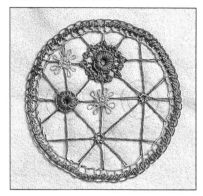

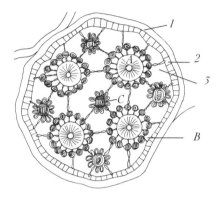

Copy the pattern illustrated.
Couch a tt around the outer
circle (1).
Line the circle with a single row of
extended tbs (2) hooped over the tt.
Next, couch paired threads along
the grid of squares and diagonals as
shown (3), whipping the outer ends
through the loops of 2 from one
position to the next.
There are now 4 points where 8
paired threads intersect (A).
Oversew these crossings to make a
central hole at each, marking the
position of future rings (4).
Around A, knot a sewing thread, B,
to each of the 8 grid threads, to
make a circle. Go round again,
weaving knobs at each intersection,
and also in between (total 16). For
the intermediate knobs, a 3rd spoke
is made by taking the thread down
to A, passing it around the
oversewing, then weaving in and
out of these 3 threads.

There are 5 points, C, where 4
paired threads intersect. Here,
work square-shaped woven knobs,
with a pair of loop picots in each
quadrant (total 8).
Pad the outer circle, 1, and hold the
padding to the tt with spaced dbs.

Woven knobs These are an
innovation, not found in any of the
earlier needlelaces. They occur
frequently in point de gaze. To
make a woven knob, simply weave
in and out of the spokes until a
rounded knob has been formed.

POINT DE GAZE 6

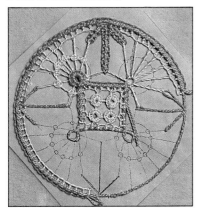

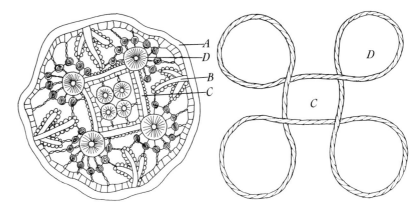

Copy the pattern illustrated and fix it to the support with self-adhesive acetate film. All tts are double.
Couch a tt around the circle A.
Couch a tt around the arrow head B, around the central square (C) and the rings (D).
Line tt A with a single row of extended tbs with a whipped return, taking the sts behind the arrow heads.
Attach the sewing thread to the tt of one of the rings (D). Carry it across to the inner end of the arrow shaft (B) and back again, twisting as you go. Take the thread around tt D, out to one of the points of the arrow head, and back to D. In this way attach a total of 9 twisted strands as shown, looping the 5 middle ones over A.
Repeat this procedure for each ring.
Beginning at X, on the square, knot a thread to each of the 9 strands and to Y.
Work back again, weaving a knob over each knot.

Line the tt of C with tbs. Do not whip over the loops.
Starting from C, cross the interior of the square with a grid of paired threads, whipping through the loops of the tbs lining to link one line of the grid to the next. Separate the threads where they cross, and buttonhole closely around this hole to make a small ring.

Pad the outline of C with 3 strands of coton perlé, and bind them to the tt with spaced dbs.
At the same time, pad the rings (D) and buttonhole closely over them.
Surround the arrow heads with a line of knotted sts with arched loops, taking each st around the double tt.
Lay 3 padding strands of coton perlé over A, and attach this padding to the tt by spaced dbs.

POINT DE GAZE 7

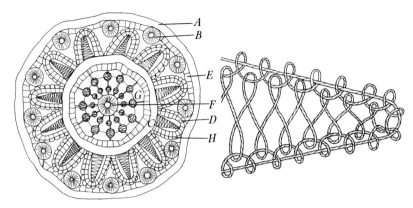

Copy the pattern and attach it to the support with self-adhesive acetate film. In the sample, diameters have been drawn as guide lines.

Couch tts around the 2 circles A and C.

Couch tt around the 12 equal-sized triangles D that project from C like fangs.

Line A and C with a row of tbs E. Go around again, whipping through the loops.

Sling 12 long lightly-twisted sts from the lining layer of C, almost to the centre, holding their inner ends in position with couching sts. Run the sewing thread in and out of their inner portions to make a light padding, then buttonhole closely over the padding to form a ring, F.

Link the 12 radii together by knotting 2 concentric circles of sewing thread to them. Work a raised knob over each knot G.

Outline the core of the fangs with

sewing thread and work a row of dbs all the way around the inside, pointing the needle inwards. Needleweave the thread between opposing loops to fill the central space (I). Each time, before tightening the thread, place the needle in position for the next st. Lay padding strands over C, and bind them to the tt with spaced dbs.

Frame the outer border of every tooth with a line of knotted stitches separated by arched loops (H). Alternating with the fangs are 12 rings, formed by running padding strands through tt A and the layer of tbs that lines it. Buttonhole closely over the padding with the needle pointing outwards.

Alternatively the rings can be made independently, see Argentella 8. Attach the ring to the lace with small stab sts.

Lay padding strands over A and bind the padding to the tt with spaced dbs.

Point de gaze collar

Most of the elements were made as already described in chapter two, but because of their large size it was necessary to support the working threads by the lavish use of couching stitches. The attached petals were made separately. Stitch 2A was slightly modified.

Threads

The threads used were as follows: coton à broder 16 and 20 in shades of écru. A double strand of 16 was used for the tt, and 4 strands for the cordonnet, divided into 2 and 2 as necessary, for the 'return trips'.

The design of this collar, which was worked by Joan Carter, is based on modes copied directly from the 19th-century flounce.

A point de gaze flower with two raised petals, worked separately and then stitched in position.

inner raised petal

outer raised petal

basic flower shape

dbs

point de gaze ground

7

5

2A

6

CHAPTER 3

DESIGNS: TRADITIONAL AND ONWARDS

This chapter is about making a transition from the designs, threads and textures of antique laces to your own personal and original form of self-expression.

How can you begin? We asked a number of leading textile artists about their own experiences in creative needlelace – what was the source of their inspiration, and the aim of their production? What governed their decisions on form, colour, stitch, raised work, and added decorations? Their fascinating revelations follow this brief introduction. You will notice the variety of their approaches to composition, and their imaginative freedom.

In the first two chapters, we examined in detail the work of antique lacemakers. Bearing in mind that they were professionals, needing to earn their living, they were bound by market restrictions imposed by designers and traders. However, there is still much to be learned from them about the order of working, the laying of the tracing thread, the interlocking of all threads to make a stable fabric, fitting the stitches into a space of awkward shape, disposing of loose ends, how and where to add raised embellishments, and the final detachment of the lace from the pattern. Although today there is no longer any obligation to abide by rigid rules, the discipline of practising and perfecting stitch formations is still as essential a preliminary to true creativity as the brick or concrete foundations on which many different styles of architecture are based.

New departures can begin as random doodles, or as organized designs. Doodles have the advantage that they require no real skill in composition drawing. You can experiment with coloured areas by scribbling in crayon or paint; with textures by varying shades of grey. Much the simplest method is computer graphics, which are not only rapid to create but can with equal swiftness be erased or altered,

Silver Brooch *by Pat Gibson. Pat's work has been influenced by point de gaze, with its layering of petals. Here, she used silver, silk and rayon machine-embroidery threads, with added silver beads and wire.*

Summer of Content *by Wilcke Smith*

while at the same time your several versions can be either printed out or saved, so that you can return to them later if other ideas for their use occur to you.

Once you have found a pleasing shape, examine it from the practical point of view. Can a supporting (tracing) thread conveniently be couched around it? What stitches would fit into the various enclosures you have made, and have you left sufficient room for them? When you are satisfied that all is well you can make your pattern, and begin the work, following the basic procedures already described.

Making a new design

Designs begin with a sketch. If you have little experience in drawing, and are nervous about your ability, begin by copying. The designs for the seven projects shown in the last chapter were copied more or less faithfully from the antique laces. You can do the same: select a motif from an actual lace and draw it, or trace its outline from a photograph or photocopy. Incidentally, while antique laces are fair game, you should not copy a contemporary lacemaker's original design without her consent, unless of course it is presented for that purpose.

Copying or tracing need not be restricted to laces. The needlelace-makers of Youghal at first used designs intended for porcelain. Old journals of needlecraft, or engravings of fashion accessories intended to be worked in surface embroidery, can provide many ideas. Flowers and animals can be copied in their natural or idealized form, or you might trace an outline from a natural history picture or postcard. Once you have a drawing that you like, it can be enlarged or reduced by photocopier or, more laboriously, by scaling it up on graph paper.

Points to consider
As you make your design, so you need to consider its *purpose*. Will it be practical or pictorial, flat or a three-dimensional 'sculpture'? Many small, simple motifs can be adapted for collars, brooches, purses, or handkerchief corners, for example.

Skeletal Leaf, *by embroiderer and calligrapher Joan Carter, is a pleasing idea, its simple concept demonstrating how inspiration can be found in the most familiar of everyday objects. A fallen leaf, reduced to a network of veins by the rotting away of its fleshier substance, is rendered in tawny silks within a tracing-thread outline of fine flexible wire.*

If your design is symmetrical, draw one side; photocopy it on to tracing paper; turn the tracing paper over; fix it carefully in position to make a mirror image, and then photocopy the whole.

It is at this stage that stitches should be indicated on your design. Mark in their numbers (or names) in pencil, in case you change your mind later. If you wish the form of the design to remain dominant, make sure that it will not be overpowered by the stitches you have chosen. Look again at the antique laces, and notice how they achieved their own balance.

Threads also need to be considered before you begin on the lace itself. Thread and texture are closely linked, and if you are working out your own ideas the decisions about threads are among the most difficult to make. It is excellent advice to try out a sample of each stitch in the thread that you would like to use. See how it works – it may be too thick, making the stitches over-large for the allocated area, or too thin, providing insufficient substance. Useful everyday threads are coton à broder 16 and Gutermann or Madeira silks 100/3.

Once you are happy that the design, the purpose, the stitches and the thread will all blend together, copy the design to make the pattern. Keep the design for reference, bearing in mind that the pattern will become gradually obscured by stitches as the work proceeds.

Second thoughts

Mistakes or errors of procedure may be very difficult and time-consuming to alter. Refer back to the basic techniques before actually beginning the lace. If you are new to needlelace, keep your first piece simple. You may not be entirely happy with it, but don't throw your mistakes away – keep them as reminders of what went wrong, and of what you would like to alter if you were to work that design again. Even the most experienced creative lacemakers have to proceed by trial and error, sometimes reworking a part of the design several times over with different threads, stitch sizes or tensions. It's all part of the joy of creation. If you are contemplating a large piece, try dividing it into small areas that can be worked separately and fitted together later. In this way, if anything goes wrong, only individual parts will need to be altered.

Be prepared to experiment all the time. Try insects, mice or clusters of flowers. Their small areas require only a few stitches and are quick to make. Try using fine rustproof wire instead of a tracing thread to make wings, ears or petals stand out. The wire can be bent at will to give a curvy effect. You might pad their bodies with cotton wool or some similar wadding.

Combining needlelace with other techniques

Pure needlelace is notoriously slow to work, and few people these days have limitless hours to spare. A combination of needlelace with other techniques can save a great deal of time. Surface embroidery, using large stitches, can speed the work of producing a needlelace picture. In Nenia Lovesey's *Garden Gate* perspective has been created by working the embroidery on two levels – the gate and the path beyond. Pictures that consist mainly of embroidery can be over-stitched in parts with needlelace techniques, providing, for example, an impression of ridged earth, or of dappled sunlight beneath trees. An added advantage here is that tracing threads need not be used; the buttonhole stitches are no longer totally detached from the surface, and can even be anchored through the fabric at either end of every row. (Whether such work is still lace is a moot point.)

A thin wash of paint, as in the silk embroideries of the early 19th century, can provide an attractive background which is not only labour-saving, but concentrates the attention on the central image. Some of the pictures featured here have painted backgrounds.

Fabric appliqué also combines well with needlelace and is perhaps most effective in three-dimensional padded work, as in Wilcke Smith's *Cloud Sweepers*, and Barbara Hirst's *Samurai Two*.

You might also like to experiment with attached embellishments. The extremely slow-to-work embellishments of cordonnets and crowns that are characteristic of traditional needlelaces have been replaced in more modern works by natural objects, such as shells, coral and mica, or artefacts or pottery, glass or gilded paper, again with an enormous saving of time and effort. Such additions must be carefully planned to enhance the composition as a whole.

Garden Gate *by Nenia Lovesey*

108

Needlelace art

NENIA LOVESEY

A pioneer of the revival of needlelaces in the United Kingdom, and Founder and Life President of the Guild of Needlelaces, Nenia Lovesey is a child of a lacemaking family, and her approach is very versatile. The trapunto trees in *Garden Gate* were 'covered with freestyle needlelace stitches. French and bullion knots were textured together to form the path and foreground, the trunks of the trees were worked in stem stitch.' *Fire* was inspired by magnified action pictures of cigarette ash cooling.

'Shisha work was used to convey the glint of reflected light; the round raised shapes were made of wadding covered by silk, worked over with needlelace stitches, crochet, and beads covered with needleweaving. French knots, bugles and woven wheels made up the rest of the design, with braids of Ardenza stitch . . . to give the effect of smoke.'

Fire *by Nenia Lovesey*

CATHERINE BARLEY

A teacher of needlelace for the City and Guilds examinations, and Chairman of the Guild of Needlelaces from 1983 to 1989, Catherine Barley admits to a love of the traditional, but is nevertheless the creator of some delightful three-dimensional plant forms.

Pea Pods was inspired by 'the most wonderful wood carving I had ever seen. There were garlands of flowers, fruit, game birds, acanthus leaves, peapods, and even a cravat of Venetian gros point lace.' Captivated by the beauty and detail of this sensitive sculpture, she felt impelled to attempt a similar feat in lace.

The peas, pods and leaves were worked in dbs with a straight return, using 100/3 silk, in shades of green. The flower was worked in pea stitch (similar to point de Sedan 4, but replacing tbs with dbs) using Unity 150 industrial thread; and the butterfly in 160 Egyptian thread. Each piece was made separately and the outside edges stiffened with a line of horsehair over the tracing thread. A thin twig was used to support the tendrils.

Pea Pods *by Catherine Barley*

ANN COLLIER

Chairman of the Lace Guild from 1981 to 1982 and President of the *Organisation Internationale de la Dentelle au Fuseau et à l'Aiguille* (OID FA) from 1983 to 1988, Ann Collier specializes in fans, and has made 40 of them, creating her own dramatic designs within their testing semi-circular framework. Inspiration for her work has come from many sources – natural, architectural and abstract. The idea for the opulently ornate *Brighton Pavilion*, shown here, came from a sepia photograph discovered during the International Festival of Lace held in Brighton in 1986. The chosen colours of the cotton, silk and metallic threads echo this theme. The pavilion is worked in needle-lace, against a background of bobbin lace stitches.

Brighton Pavilion *by Ann Collier*

GUNNEL TEITEL

A New Yorker, Gunnel Teitel has been interested in needlelace
techniques for many years, and has worked in a variety of creative
lace and embroidery forms. *Arizona Cactus* shows the interpretation
of a simple natural effect through a sensitive eye. The variations in
stitch size, and the subtly blended colours of the raw fleece and silk
padding strands, raised against a backing of monochrome sand, give
a vivid impression of this desolately glowing desert scene.

Arizona Cactus *by Gunnel Teitel*

VIMA DEMARCHI MICHELI

Vima, from Sacramento, is the author of 25 workbooks on the needle arts, and is well known for designing contemporary uses for clothing and wall decorations. *Oriental Fish* is worked on a handwoven linen background. The traditional tts are replaced by a backstitched outline, and the rows of detached needlelace stitches are hooked through these at the end of every row.

Oriental Fish *by Vima deMarchi Micheli, stitched by Donaldine Grass*

BARBARA HIRST

Barbara Hirst is a leading exponent of that form of padded embroidery known as stumpwork, which appears to have originated in England in the first half of the 17th century. In parts, this used a looping stitch closely allied to the dbs which had long been popular for the fashionable ruffs and raised collars of the Elizabethan and early Stewart periods. Barbara has brought the technique dramatically up to date with genre representations, of jumble sales and gardening, for example, capturing in an enchanting manner the very essence of the occasion. She finds inspiration everywhere:

'Our camera is an ever useful tool for capturing basic figurative images which can be varied, as desired, by scale and clothing. Stance, posture and movement, together with suggested facial expression, are all essential prerequisites to a successful piece of work. Newspapers and magazines, the old family album with its sepia photographs, paintings, postcards and buildings have all provided inspiration for my stumpwork designs.

Subject, fabrics and threads, as well as colour, must all be matched for good effect. The rural, homespun subject is best worked in a coarse matt texture, while a subject such as *Samurai Two* has to be given splendour by a use of brilliant colour and rich metallic embellishments. 100/3 silk is the most desirable thickness, and it can be combined with finer rayon machine threads. Special effects can be achieved with space-dyed threads or by dyeing the finished piece of needlelace. The embossed samurai, mounted on a rich silk ground, has baggy trousers overworked in dbs with a straight return, using two contrasting thread colours to give a tweedy effect, and additionally patterned with surface embroidery. The lappets are attached along one border only, so that they fly free. They have a beaded wire edge and are worked in changing bands of colour and metallic gold.'

Samurai Two *by Barbara Hirst*

114

JEAN GOLDBERG

Well-known Australian fibre artist Jean Goldberg combines a vividly original imagination with a strong sense of realism. A penchant for unlikely conjunctions makes her work invariably stimulating.

'*Bird for Steve* was a wedding present for my son, a lyrebird looking sideways being the emblem of Steve's folk-dancing group. The bush surround became the supporting motif, with white eucalyptus trees in the distance relating both to the vertical edges of the composition, and to the lines of the tail. On the right, the curves of the tree-fern fronds balance those of the lyre feathers, and their plumed crowns relate to the tail, while emphasizing the bush setting. I used fine wool to give the softness of the temperate rain forest, fleece under the lace stitches of the tree-fern trunks, and cotton Retors 80 to give crispness to the feathers and their spines.

    Hi Countdown started with a handful of broken audio-cassette tape. Could it be used as thread? The theme should refer to music. An old music stand set the format by providing the mount. The first panel showed the popular dead-pan presenter "Molly" Meldrum, with cassette-tape hair. The next two panels are abstracts drawn while I was listening to the music. The fourth, *Video*, transposes eyes and mouth in the face, and old diamanté form spotlights in the right upper corner. The bottom panel is called *Singers on the Charts*. Streamers of cassette tape move in the air as viewers pass. The panels are mounted on handmade paper over board with the surround of the *Singers* painted.'

Bird for Steve *by Jean Goldberg*

Hi Countdown
by Jean Goldberg

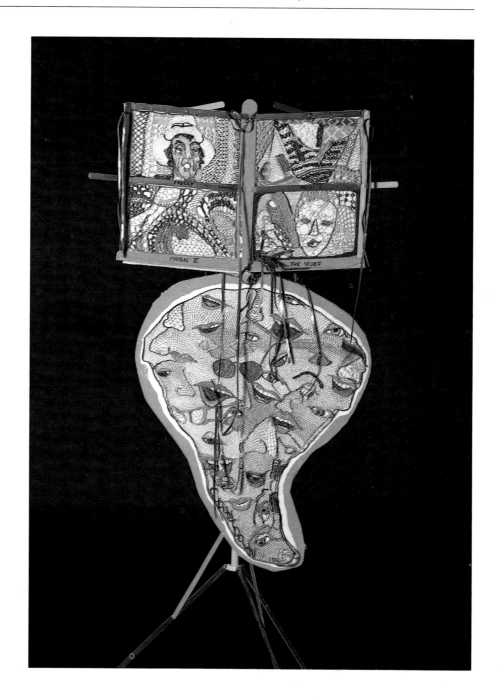

WILCKE SMITH

Wilcke Smith from New Mexico has won awards in many shows.

'Space, time and ancient cultures are important sources of imagery for me. Much knowledge of past ages comes to us in obscure shapes, undeciphered marks, and curious symbols imbued with magic.

Fibre is such a luxurious medium that its multitude of textures, materials and techniques demands discipline and limitations. Concept must be the starting point. Without an initial dream and a firm direction it is hard to compose a design that, for instance, expresses a certain landscape, sings of pure colour, or hints at an arcane message. But once the purpose is clear, colour becomes of prime importance. It can be beautiful or shocking, but it must psychologically stimulate in the direction of the initial concept.

I am prone to intricate textures, diverse embellishments, and innumerable stitches overlaid to produce iridescent blends of colour. Hence I seek strong, controlled basic forms to sustain this abundance of texture. A limited number of stitch forms – sometimes only one – emphasizes the design and underplays the aspect of embroidery per se. My purpose is to enhance the medium, edging it away from the display of a stitch for its own sake, towards stitches put to use in the art of expression.

In *Cloud Sweepers*, the two needlelace figures were stitched directly onto amate bark paper, the stitches being taken over padding of several layers of felt. The clouds were worked in silk satin stitch, within a hoop of fabric. Their shapes were cut in the amate, and the fabric mounted from behind. A few French knots in wool produced a transition around the clouds. The amate was toned with Prismacolor pencil. The sweeping brooms were wrapped, with feathered tips.

In *Summer of Content*, the vibrant background is formed of flower shapes machine-zigzagged in a variety of fabrics – velour, cotton and Thai silk – then cut out and appliquéd to the background of yellow-gold velour. The 7-inch tall figures are hooped on linen and worked in needlelace stitches using Indian rayon threads, then attached to the velvet with acid-free glue.'

Cloud Sweepers *by Wilcke Smith*

SHEILA ASHBY

Sheila Ashby lived for a number of years in the United States, and several of her works are in American museums. After a training in art and embroidery, she studied needlelace under the acclaimed creative textile artist, Virginia Churchill Bath. Sheila's own bias was always towards the use of fibre art as an original expression of ideas and emotions, rather than as an imitation of antique forms. The idea for *Ominous Sea and Sparkling Sea* began when she was asked to produce a work on the theme of fish, for an exhibition.

'That subject had no great appeal, and I decided to use the fish's environment instead. It was also an attempt to contrast two moods, using opposing colours, and also stitching the waves in one sea downwards and in the other upwards to create a livelier feeling. The detached buttonhole stitch was worked throughout in silk, the straight return threads being a different colour. Buttonholed loops were used in the sparkling sea to suggest foam, and a slight three-dimensional effect was produced by layering the waves.'

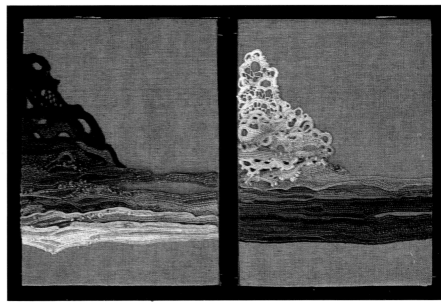

Ominous Sea and Sparkling Sea *by Sheila Ashby*

ROS HILLS

Ros Hills is noted for her brilliantly coloured compositions which erupt spontaneously from an inner melange of childhood recollections – the desert sands of Iraq, the Moghul majesty of India, the bright Caribbean jungles – into a totally abstract overt expression.

I am Woman *by Ros Hills*

'It was in these countries that I spent my formative years, absorbing colours, sounds, smells, shapes and textures into my subconscious brain. *Summer in India* epitomizes for me all the razzle dazzle and excitement of an Indian market – one named after the romantic princess Anarkali, who killed herself out of love for a prince who married another. To incorporate these images into my work I have used hot colours redolent of the aggressive sunlight of Eastern countries, as well as metallic papers, vividly coloured silk threads, and sequins mounted on a paper collage.

I am Woman is a cap, like those worn by Indian women. Its colours symbolize all the hope and joy at the beginning of the complex experience called being a woman. I prefer to use very simple needlelace techniques, relying on thread colour and texture rather than on a hundred different stitch formations. The actual working of the needlelace fabric I find tedious and exacting, but to take a single thread and create with it a fabric will always fascinate me, and will I am sure always be a part of my life.'

Summer in India *by Ros Hills*

OLWYN SCOTT

Olwyn Scott inherited her love of the renowned wild flowers of Western Australia from her botanist father, and her skill in design from her artist mother. An investigative streak led from an early interest in china painting and embroidery to a passionate curiosity about the making of lace. *Pigmy Possum on Eucalyptus Blossoms* won the overall prize in the Australian Lace Guild Awards in 1989.

'The possum was enchanting – its body no bigger than my thumb, its tail gripping tightly, the daintiest little hands, long whiskers, large translucent ears, big eyes – exquisite! Drawing the possum was difficult, especially the hands. For help, I borrowed books and pictures from all sources. Eventually I decided that the eyes, ears and tail were the most important features and a crouching position would hide the hands. I draw from specimen whenever possible.

Having decided on the essential characteristics and basic lines, I draw, keeping in mind balance, focal point, proportion and so on, and my art teacher's three golden rules for design, "Simplify, simplify, simplify". Most successful designs look simple – seldom is it obvious that much time has been expended. I felt that possum deserved to look as natural as possible, so I chose needlelace, as it allows for detail, control of line, texture, and flexibility of working.

In this piece the subject, possum, decided the type of lace and its end use – pictorial. At other times it is the finished article which determines the size, shape and thus the lace. Each lace has its own limitations which challenge the designer. Colour in lace can detract from the design. I use colour only when it is the essential characteristic which differentiates the subject from other similar shapes.

I think if I worked possum again I would work all the stems and leaves underneath first, and mount her slightly elevated, maybe even padded, with the tail "in the round" like the stems. The ears could be wired to stand out from the body . . .'

The possum is mounted on a midnight blue backing, since left unsupported the slender stems would coil and twist upon themselves.

Pigmy Possum on Eucalyptus Blossoms *by Olwyn Scott*

VIRGINIA CHURCHILL BATH

The theme of three-dimensional fantasy also appears in the spectacular works of Virginia Churchill Bath, who served on the staff of the Art Institute of Chicago from 1952 to 1971. Her many varied lace creations, sometimes in the form of garments, huge wall hangings, or openwork structures supported on plexiglass, make skilful use of varied needlelace stitches in linen, cotton, wool and silk, combined with relief embroidery and inclusions of wood, ceramic, amethyst or shells to produce monumental near-sculptural effects.

Bagatelle (detail), worked in 1990, incorporates both needle and bobbin lace techniques, using not only linen, cotton, synthetic and metallic threads, cords and yarns, but also linen cloth, wood, metal and mica.

Foam (detail), worked in 1971, combines needlelace with embroidery and machine work. Wood, wire and shells were used, in addition to cotton and linen threads.

Foam *by Virginia Churchill Bath*

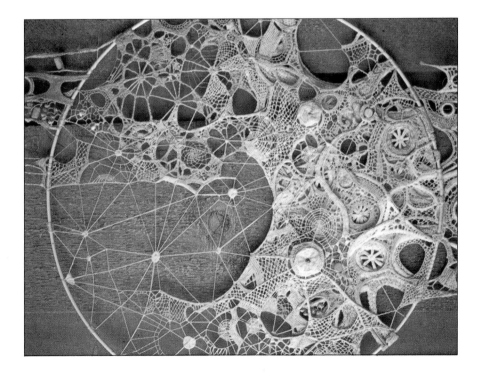

Bagatelle *by Virginia Churchill Bath*

ELIZABETH ELLSWORTH

Elizabeth Ellsworth of New York specializes in, and teaches, needle-lace jewellery using basic stitches. Her students are encouraged to explore the qualities of different fibres and threads, particularly those with body and richness, such as shiny twisted silks, rayons, nylons, velvety velours and sparkling metallics, as well as the more usual pearl cottons, crochet threads and linen. She offers ideas and guidelines to her students, but urges them to interpret these ideas in individual ways, adding beads, shisha mirrors, feathers, or whatever else may spark their imagination.

Pendant *by Elizabeth Ellsworth*

INDEX

Acetate
  pattern, supporting 12
Alençon lace 74–83
  brides tortillées 74, 81
  characteristics 74
  designs 76–81
  development of 7
  filling stitches 74
  O à nez en chainettes 80
  O en chainettes 80
  project 82, 83
  réseau ordinaire ground 74, 81
  shadow effect 75
  tulle 74
Architect's linen 13
Argentan lace 59–61
  brides bouclées 52, 59
  brides tortillées 52
  brode 59
  characteristics 52
  cordonnet 59
  designs 54–9
  development of 7, 52
  flower centres 58
  project 60, 61
  réseau ordinaire 52
  réseau rosacé ground 52
Argentella lace 62–73
  characteristics 62
  circles 66, 71
  designs 64–71
  development of 7, 62
  flower centres 70
  hexagons 68, 69
  mouches 64
  octagons 66
  project 72, 73
  réseau ordinaire 66
  réseau rosacé ground 67
  squares 71
Assembly 26

Brides bouclées 52, 59
Brides tortillées
  Alençon lace 74, 81
  Argentan lace 52
Brode 14, 27, 59
Brussels needlelace 86, 91

Centres of manufacture
  Flanders 7
  France 7
  Sedan 7
  Venice 6
Collars
  child's, Point de Sedan 50, 51
  Point de gaze 102, 103
Cordonnet 14, 15, 27
  Argentan 59
  Point de gaze 94
  Point de France 44
Crowns
  Point de France 40

Decorative fillings 14, 15, 23, 24
Designs
  mistakes in 107
  new, making 106–8
  solid areas 19
Despierres, Mme 14
Detached buttonhole stitch 6, 19
Direction of working 18

Embellishments 25
  attached 108

Filling stitches, *see* Decorative fillings
Finishing 27
Flanders, style in 7
France, style in 7

Gauze lace, *see* Point de gaze
Ground 14, 15

History of Alençon Lace 14

Imitations 8
Ireland
  design schools 11

Jours 14

Knotted buttonhole stitch 97

Loose ends 22

Mistakes, correcting 22
Modes 14, 15
Mouches 64

Needlelace
  centres of manufacture 6, 7
  embroidery, transition from 29
  imitations 8
  meaning 6
  modern 9
  order of working 14
  other techniques, combined with 108
  outline, laying 16, 17
Needles 10

Outline, laying 16, 17
Overtwisting 10

Patterns
  backing 13
  designs 11
  protecting 12, 13
  supporting 12, 13
Picots, types of 39, 41, 78
Point de France 7, 30–43
  cordonnet 41
  creation of 30
  crowns 40

Point de France – *cont.*
   designs 32–41
   ground 39
   portes 32
   project 42, 43
   ring picots 41
Point de gaze 7, 94–103
   characteristics 94
   cordonnet 94
   designs 96–101
   flower 102
   knotted buttonhole stitch 97
   project 102, 103
   Zele needlelace, traditions carried
     on by 94
Point de Sedan 44–51
   characteristics 44, 45
   designs 46–9
   peastitch 48
   petit mignon 48
   project 50, 51
   sleeve ruffle 45
Pricker 11, 13
Punto in aria 7, 8, 29

Relief 25, 27
Rempli 14

Réseau Venise 84–93
   characteristics 84
   chevrons 90
   designs 86–91
   double diamonds 89
   origin of 7
   project 92, 93
   réseau ordinaire with rings 86
   solid diamonds 89
   stitches in every row 87
   tilted squares 90
   triangles in hexagons 91

S-direction 18
Samples, working 20, 21
Sedan 7, 44
Snarling 10
Solid design areas 19
Stitches
   detached buttonhole stitch 6,
     19
   filling 23, 24
   knotted buttonhole stitch 97
   petit mignon 48
   protecting 12
   twisted buttonhole stitch 23, 24
Stumpwork 114

Threads
   broder 10
   buttonholing over cordonnet, for
     27
   considering 107
   coton perlé 10
   cotton 10
   silks 10
   snarling 10
   tracing 7, 16, 17
Tulle 74
Twisted buttonhole stitch 23,
   24

Venice 6

Working
   direction of 18
   ground 25
   order of 14
   samples 20–2
Woven knobs 98

Z-direction 18, 19
Zele lace 14
   Point de gaze traditions 94

FOR FURTHER INFORMATION

Merehurst is the leading publisher of craft books and has an excellent range of titles to suit all levels.
Please send for our free catalogue, stating the title of this book:–

UNITED KINGDOM
Publicity Department
Merehurst Ltd.
Ferry House
51–57 Lacy Road
London SW15 1PR
Tel: 081 780 1177
Fax: 081 780 1714

UNITED STATES OF AMERICA
Sterling Publishing Co. Inc.
387 Park Avenue South
New York NY 10016–8810
USA
Tel: (1) 212 532 7160
Fax: (1) 212 213 2495

AUSTRALIA
J. B. Fairfax Press Pty. Ltd.
80 McLachlan Avenue
Rushcutters Bay
NSW 2011
Tel: (61) 2 361 6366
Fax: (61) 2 360 6262

OTHER TERRITORIES
For further information contact:
Merehurst International Sales
Department at *United Kingdom*
address